I0414042

Editor-in-Chief and Founder:
  Lyndon H. LaRouche, Jr.
Editorial Board: *Lyndon H. LaRouche, Jr. , Helga
  Zepp-LaRouche, Robert Ingraham, Tony
  Papert, Gerald Rose, Dennis Small, Jeffrey
  Steinberg, William Wertz*
Co-Editors: *Robert Ingraham, Tony Papert*
Managing Editor: *Nancy Spannaus*
Technology: *Marsha Freeman*
Books: *Katherine Notley*
Ebooks: *Richard Burden*
Graphics: *Alan Yue*
Photos: *Stuart Lewis*
Circulation Manager: *Stanley Ezrol*

INTELLIGENCE DIRECTORS
Counterintelligence: *Jeffrey Steinberg, Michele
  Steinberg*
Economics: *John Hoefle, Marcia Merry Baker,
  Paul Gallagher*
History: *Anton Chaitkin*
Ibero-America: *Dennis Small*
Russia and Eastern Europe: *Rachel Douglas*
United States: *Debra Freeman*

INTERNATIONAL BUREAUS
Bogotá: *Miriam Redondo*
Berlin: *Rainer Apel*
Copenhagen: *Tom Gillesberg*
Houston: *Harley Schlanger*
Lima: *Sara Madueño*
Melbourne: *Robert Barwick*
Mexico City: *Gerardo Castilleja Chávez*
New Delhi: *Ramtanu Maitra*
Paris: *Christine Bierre*
Stockholm: *Ulf Sandmark*
United Nations, N.Y.C.: *Leni Rubinstein*
Washington, D.C.: *William Jones*
Wiesbaden: *Göran Haglund*

ON THE WEB
e-mail: eirns@larouchepub.com
www.larouchepub.com
www.executiveintelligencereview.com
www.larouchepub.com/eiw
Webmaster: *John Sigerson*
Assistant Webmaster: *George Hollis*
Editor, Arabic-language edition: *Hussein Askary*

EIR (ISSN 0273-6314) *is published weekly
(50 issues), by EIR News Service, Inc.,
P.O. Box 17390, Washington, D.C. 20041-0390.
(703) 297-8434*

European Headquarters: E.I.R. GmbH, Postfach
Bahnstrasse 9a, D-65205, Wiesbaden, Germany
Tel: 49-611-73650
Homepage: http://www.eir.de
e-mail: info@eir.de
Director: Georg Neudecker

Montreal, Canada: 514-461-1557
eir@eircanada.ca

Denmark: EIR - Danmark, Sankt Knuds Vej 11,
basement left, DK-1903 Frederiksberg, Denmark.
Tel.: +45 35 43 60 40, Fax: +45 35 43 87 57. e-mail:
eirdk@hotmail.com.

Mexico City: EIR, Sor Juana Inés de la Cruz 242-2
Col. Agricultura C.P. 11360
Delegación M. Hidalgo, México D.F.
Tel. (5525) 5318-2301
eirmexico@gmail.com

Canada Post Publication Sales Agreement
#40683579

Postmaster: Send all address changes to *EIR*, P.O.
Box 17390, Washington, D.C. 20041-0390.

Signed articles in *EIR* represent the views of the authors,
and not necessarily those of the Editorial Board.

Mankind Transforms Himself

EDITORIAL

A Radical Change in Trans-Atlantic Axioms Must Be Accepted

by Robert Ingraham

May 15, 2017—Increasingly, since August 1971, the nations and populations of the "western" world have become dominated by the axioms of the British Empire. To wit, these include:

- Buy cheap, sell dear,
- A disregard for human life,
- Permanent Warfare,
- Free Trade,
- Worship of a mythological "primitive" state of nature,
- The pursuit of hedonistic pleasure.

This is not a natural state of human affairs. These are not the ideas, nor are they representative of the philosophy upon which western civilization was created. These are the axioms of the 18th, 19th and 20th century British Empire. These are the axioms of Bertrand Russell, H.G. Wells and the House of Windsor, failed axioms which fly in the face of the tangible evidence of lawful human development. These are also the same axioms which have led to the subjugation of the trans-Atlantic world by a monetarist elite. During the recent decades, particularly under the 2001-2017 Bush/Obama regime, these perversions of human culture have come to permeate every level of our society, our government institutions, and our media.

As reports from the May 14-15 Beijing Belt and Road Forum stream in, it is now irrefutable that a new dynamic, a new vision for humanity—one contrary to the bankrupt policies and outlook of the past forty years—has been unleashed onto the global stage, one grounded in human development, cooperation, opportunity, and peace. A pathway out from our present existentialist dead-end has been presented—for all to see and to join with.

Yet, many well-intentioned inhabitants of Europe and the Americas seem incapable of perceiving, much as was E.A. Poe's fictional Police Prefect G——, that which lies in plain sight.

Will the inhabitants and the political leaders of the United States and the European Union recognize this opportunity? Will they break through their delusions and self-limiting obsessions—their political and personal agendas that are fixed in perpetual motion by their faulty axioms—long enough to recognize the great turning-point in human history that has now been offered to all of mankind? Will they act on this?

A Pregnant Moment

In a May 14 interview with the Chinese news service Xinhua, Helga Zepp-LaRouche, President of the German Schiller Institute, stated, "The Belt and Road Initiative is the most important strategic initiative on the planet. It not only brings economic prosperity to all participating countries, but also serves as a true basis for a peace order for the 21st Century."

On the day after this interview, Mrs. LaRouche addressed a think-tank summit associated with the Belt and Road Forum. Her speech, titled "The Belt and Road becomes the World Land-Bridge," included the following:

Heads of State and Heads of Government at the opening session of the Belt and Road Forum, May 14, 2017.

There has been a breathtaking dynamic of the New Silk Road in the three and a half years since it was pronounced by President Xi Jinping in 2013. The Belt and Road Initiative (BRI) has the obvious potential of quickly becoming a World Land-Bridge, connecting all continents through infrastructure, such as tunnels and bridges, reinforced by the Maritime Silk Road. As such, it represents a new form of globalization, but not determined by the criteria of profit maximization for the financial sector, but for the harmonious development of all participating countries on the basis of "win-win" cooperation.

It is therefore important, that one does not look at the BRI from the standpoint of an accountant, who projects his statistical viewpoint of cost-benefit into the future, but that we think about it as a Vision for the Community of a Shared Future.

Precisely! It is this reality of a Vision for the Community of a Shared Future which was front-and-center in Beijing. The final Joint Communique issued by the participants at the forum, including almost thirty heads of state or government, stressed exactly this view, and many of the speakers spoke directly to the "new future"

which is now being created.

Russian President Vladimir Putin, in his speech to the forum, stated,

> I would like to stress that Russia does not simply view the future of the Eurasian partnership as the mere establishment of new ties between states and economies. This partnership must shift the political and economic landscape of the continent and bring peace, stability, prosperity, and a new quality of life to Eurasia.
>
> In this respect, the greater Eurasia is not an abstract geopolitical arrangement but, without exaggeration, a truly civilization-wide project looking toward the future.
>
> I believe that by maintaining the spirit of cooperation, we can achieve that future. I want to thank President Xi Jinping for this well-timed initiative, promising such splendid prospects for cooperation.

While Chinese President Xi Jinping, the host of the forum, situated the intent of the gathering thus:

> We should build the Belt and Road into a road for peace. The ancient silk routes thrived in times of peace, but lost vigor in times of war. The pursuit of the Belt and Road Initiative requires a peaceful and stable environment. We should foster a new type of international relations featuring win-win cooperation; and we should forge partnerships of dialogue with no confrontation and of friendship rather than alliance. All countries should respect each other's sovereignty, dignity and territorial integrity, each other's development paths and social systems, and each other's core interests and major concerns....
>
> We should build the Belt and Road into a road of prosperity. Development holds the master key to solving all problems. In pursuing the Belt and Road Initiative, we should focus on the fundamental issue of development, release the growth potential of various countries, and achieve economic integration and inter-

connected development, and deliver benefits to all. . . .

We should build the Belt and Road into a road connecting different civilizations. In pursuing the Belt and Road Initiative, we should ensure that when it comes to different civilizations, exchange will replace estrangement, mutual learning will replace clashes, and coexistence will replace a sense of superiority. This will boost mutual understanding, mutual respect, and mutual trust among different countries.

Representatives for more than half of the world's peoples participated in the Belt and Road Forum. Multiple billions of dollars of infrastructure and other development projects are already under construction. This is the new future we all desire.

Some, within both the European Union and the United States, recognize the critical importance of this juncture. Recent actions by President Trump and Secretary of State Tillerson to improve relations with both China and Russia are indicative of this. President Trump's decision to send Matthew Pottinger, head of the East Asia Bureau of the National Security Council and Special Advisor to the President, to the Beijing Forum, is another sign of the shift now taking place. In Europe as well, there are voices of sanity. But the heavy hand of London's oligarchs and their stooges in Europe and the United States is omnipresent in their efforts to prevent the magnitude of this opportunity from being known to the citizens of these nations. The anti-human role being played by the *New York Times* and like-minded publications in Europe is central to their efforts.

In comments to colleagues on May 15, Lyndon LaRouche stressed: "China is doing a good job. China is placing itself in the front of the development dynamic." And this dynamic is one that will not be easily sidetracked. Were the nations of Europe and the Americas to enthusiastically enlist in the effort, it will become unstoppable. However—the ultimate orientation of America and the nations of Europe toward this New Paradigm remains, as of this moment, unresolved. The great weakness in the situation is the cultural decay within the trans-Atlantic world.

LaRouche's Challenge

With his destruction of the social democrat Abba Lerner during a debate at Queens College in 1971,

Lyndon LaRouche emerged as the paramount champion of physical (human) economics, and the leading strategic threat to the murderous monetarist practices of the City of London and their lap-dogs on Wall Street and elsewhere.

Beginning with his proposal for an International Development Bank in 1975, and continuing now for more than forty years, LaRouche has waged an unceasing fight for global financial and economic reform. This has included the 1992 proposal for a Eurasian Land-Bridge—an initiative taken in partnership with his wife Helga—his 1997 proposal for a New Bretton Woods monetary system, and his decades-long fight for a return to the principles of Hamiltonian economics.

During this time, LaRouche has traveled all over the world, met with numerous leaders and heads of state, and delivered hundreds of speeches, articles, and interviews. Make no mistake! It is Lyndon LaRouche who has led this effort, the fruits of which we now see radiating outward from Beijing.

He has also been persecuted, vilified, and prosecuted. He spent five years in a U.S. penitentiary for his hubris in challenging the imperial power of the elites. But he never wavered, and he was never cowed; for Lyndon LaRouche has always operated from a higher principle, and it is in that realm that the solution to the current trans-Atlantic cultural problem is to be found.

Axiomatic Change

In the May 12, 2017 *EIR*, a 1999 article by Lyndon LaRouche, "How to Tell the Future" was reprinted.[1] To fully clarify the transformation which is now required among the populations of Europe and America, we quote here from sections of that article:

> Most of the time, and on most of the really important decisions you make, you rarely, if ever, actually made up your own mind. That fact, however its mention embarrasses you, is what most of the mass media, crooked politicians, and pollsters and forecasters generally rely upon, in the way in which they win their incomes from the credulity of those suckers—the majority of the population—who, in recent times, have seldom actually made up their own minds about

1. "How To Tell the Future," by Lyndon H. LaRouche, Jr., August 14, 1999, reprinted in *EIR* May 12, 2017, Vol 44 No 19

almost anything of relevance to the future of our nation and its economy.

Unless you help me wake up their sleeping minds, most people today actually know almost nothing, and will probably know even less as time passes. In place of knowing, they have adopted opinions, which, they believe, will cause other people to like them, or perhaps simply not dislike them, or even bring tangible forms of rewards, such as sex, money, and relatively higher rank in some real, or even merely imagined, social pecking-order. The popular cult of Hollywood "stars," is a leading example of this sort of widespread corruption of the population. . . .

The most notable of the general follies which have defined the predictable course of the recent thirty-odd years of U.S. history, is the disengagement of the mind of the victim, the typical citizen, from his, or her former sense of an efficient connection between his existence, and the physical reality of the economy upon which individual existence depends. This specific form of personal moral perversion was already rampant in English-speaking history, in the legacies of Thomas Hobbes and John Locke, and also in the radically irrationalist notion of the "invisible hand" adopted by the cult-followers of Bernard Mandeville and Adam Smith. . . .

The worst part of this, was not that psychological break with reality, which dominates the majority among "baby boomers," x's, and y's today. The worst part, has been the passion with which these errant minds defend those opinions and preferences which impel them to reject the physical reality of human existence, just because physical reality is seen as an alien force whose influence they must resist, even reject. Thus, cut loose from earlier, traditional moorings to sanity, the post-1964-1972 population lost its moorings within the real universe. Reality ceased to be a standard for judging which opinions were sane, and which not.

The U.S. economy and associated Bretton Woods system, as these have coexisted since the 1971 introduction of the ultimately self-doomed "floating exchange-rate monetary system," are an inherently self-doomed system, which, if their existence is continued in that form, must converge on a certain boundary-state, at which they must, in effect, be turned inward upon themselves, and destroy themselves in that way. The key to understanding that system, in particular, is to place emphasis upon the vicious discrepancy between the characteristic form of action which is built into the system, axiomatically, and the real universe on which the system acts, the universe also acting upon the system. My Triple-Curve illustration is the simplest possible representation of the way in which that tragic self-boundedness of the presently doomed system has been defined. . . .

Under such conditions, the question of survival becomes, simply, can enough people be prompted to make the necessary changes in their axiomatic assumptions, fast enough, in time, to set into motion the new, viable economic process, which is required if mankind is to be prevented from going to its doom along with the inevitably doomed, tragic old system now collapsing. The question is, can you organize your neighbor to awaken, and become sane again, in time to launch the new system, before we all go down together for failure to launch the new system in a timely fashion?

In a commencement speech delivered to graduates at Liberty University on May 13, President Donald Trump stated this challenge in his own way,

Nothing worth doing ever, ever, ever came easy. Following your convictions means you must be willing to face criticism from those who lack the same courage to do what is right—and they know what is right—but they don't have the courage . . . to take it and to do it. It's called "the road less traveled."

What will future Americans say we did in our brief time right here on Earth? Did we take risks? Did we dare to defy expectations? Did we challenge accepted wisdom? And take on established systems?

Courageous world leaders have now brought into existence precisely the "new system" which LaRouche defined in 1999. Will the people of Europe and America remain out in the cold?

EIR Contents

www.larouchepub.com Volume 44, Number 20, May 19, 2017

桌会议一 全球化新形势: 新挑战、新机遇、新对策
Roundtable I New Situation of Globalization: New Challenges,
New Opportunities, New Countermeasures
主办单位: 中国国际经济交流中心
Organizer: China Center for International Economic Exchanges
2017年5月15日 中国·北京 May 15, 2017 Beijing, China

Cover This Week

Helga Zepp-LaRouche participated in the Belt and Road Forum for International Cooperation.

Schiller Institute

HELGA ZEPP-LAROUCHE IN BEIJING

The Belt and Road Becomes The World Land-Bridge

May 15—*Helga Zepp-LaRouche, president of the Schiller Institute, Germany, delivered this speech today at the Belt and Road Forum for International Cooperation in Beijing. She was addressing Roundtable I of the Fifth Global Think Tank Summit.*

There has been a breathtaking dynamic of the New Silk Road in the three and a half years since it was announced by President Xi Jinping in 2013. The Belt and Road Initiative has the obvious potential of quickly becoming a World Land-Bridge, connecting all continents through infrastructure, such as tunnels and bridges, and reinforced by the Maritime Silk Road. As such, it represents a new form of globalization, one not determined by the criteria of profit maximization for the financial sector, but rather the harmonious development of all participating countries on the basis of Win-Win cooperation.

It is therefore important, not to look at the Belt and Road Initiative (BRI) from the standpoint of an accountant, who projects his statistical viewpoint of cost-benefit into the future, but that we instead think about it as a Vision for the Community of a Shared Future. Where do we want humanity as a whole to be in 10, 100, or even in 1,000 years? Is it not the natural destiny of mankind, as the only creative species known in the universe so far, that we will be building villages on the moon, develop a deeper understanding of the trillions of galaxies in our Universe, solve the problem of what until now have been incurable diseases, or solve the problem of energy and raw materials security through the development of thermonuclear fusion power? By focusing on the common aims of humanity, we will be able to overcome geopolitics and establish a higher level of reason for the benefit of all.

It is obvious, that the World Land-Bridge is ideal for completing the development of the landlocked areas of

Helga Zepp-LaRouche at the Belt and Road Forum for International Cooperation, May 14-15.

Schiller Institute

Schiller Institute

Helga Zepp-LaRouche, participating in the Fifth Global Think Tank Summit on the theme of promoting global growth, on May 15, 2017, during the Belt and Road Forum.

our planet. The colonization of nearby space will be the obvious next phase of infrastructural development to expand the natural habitat of man.

Looking at the world land map, the United States is not merely a country surrounded by two oceans and two neighbors, but can be a central part of an infrastructure corridor which connects the southern tip of Ibero America through Central and South America, with the Eurasian transport system via a tunnel under the Bering Strait. Since President Xi Jinping has made the offer to President Trump for the United States to join the Belt and Road Initiative, there is now a practical proposal on the table, by means of which the United States can become an integral part of the World Land-Bridge. The infrastructure requirements of the United States, which are enormous, could be a perfect opportunity to convert all or part of the $1.4 trillion that China holds in U.S. Treasury bills, into such investments via an infrastructure bank. For example, the United States really needs approximately 40,000 miles of high-speed rail lines, if it wants to match the Chinese plan to connect every large domestic Chinese city by high-speed rail by the year 2020.

The U.S. economy would experience a tremendous boost through such a grand scale of infrastructure investment, and could in turn export into the fast growing Chinese market. Once competition is replaced by cooperation, the opportunities for joint ventures between the United States and China in third countries are enormous.

Now that President Trump has declared his intension to reintroduce the American System of Economy of Al-

exander Hamilton, Henry C. Clay, and Abraham Lincoln, and to reintroduce the Glass Steagall legislation of Franklin D. Roosevelt, the possibility of an early establishment of a National Bank and a Credit System in order to channel Chinese holdings into infrastructure investments could be implemented soon.

While more and more European nations, both outside and within the EU, are recognizing the tremendous potentials of the BRI and have expressed the intension of becoming a hub for Eurasian cooperation, the EU itself has been relatively reserved, to put it diplomatically.

There is however one huge challenge, which could convince the member states of the EU to cooperate with the BRI: The refugee crisis. The only human way to heal this moral wound of Europe is for the European nations to actively integrate themselves with the BRI, into a Grand Design development plan for all of Africa.

The positive new prospect of United States-Russia de-escalation and military-to-military cooperation in Syria, along with the Astana process, now puts stabilization of the entire Southwest Asia region in sight. Offers by China to extend the New Silk Road to Southwest Asia already exist.

The New Silk Road must—as the ancient one did—lead to an exchange of the most beautiful expressions of culture of all participating countries, in order to succeed. The true meaning of Win-Win cooperation is not just the material benefit of infrastructure and industrial development, but of making the joyful discoveries of other cultures, of the beauty of their classical music, poetry, and painting, and, by knowing them, we strengthen our love for mankind as a whole.

In the building of the World Land-Bridge, all nations will cooperate on studying how to apply the laws of the Nöosphere to the establishment of durable forms of self-government. The development of the creative mental powers of all people in all nations will give all of mankind the sense of unity and purpose which will make our species truly human. When we organize our societies around scientific and artistic discovery, we will perfect our knowledge on how we can continuously advance the process of the self-development of mankind, intellectually, morally, and aesthetically, and we will find our freedom in necessity—doing our duty with passion!

Beijing Belt and Road Forum Launches 'Project of the Century'

by William Jones

May 16—The Belt and Road Forum, held in Beijing on May 14-15, brought together 29 heads of state and heads of government and over 1,500 delegates, including many heads of think-tanks dealing with the Belt and Road Initiative (BRI). Most prominent among these was Schiller Institute President Helga Zepp-LaRouche, who is considered by many Chinese scholars as the inspiration behind the project. During the conference, Mrs. Zepp-LaRouche received extensive media coverage and was well received by all the delegates. The Forum was a clear consolidation by the Chinese government of the overwhelming support for the Belt and Road Initiative by over 100 governments and international institutions.

President Xi Jinping opened the conference with a sweeping philosophical vision of what the world might look like if we reject the pettiness and intrigues of traditional geopolitics. "Over 2,000 years ago, our ancestors, trekking across vast steppes and deserts, opened the transcontinental passage connecting Asia, Europe, and Africa, known today as the Silk Road," President Xi said. "Our ancestors, navigating rough seas, created sea routes linking the East with the West, namely, the maritime Silk Road. These ancient silk routes opened windows of friendly engagement among nations, adding a splendid chapter to the history of human progress. Spanning thousands of miles and years, the ancient silk routes embody the spirit of peace and cooperation, openness and inclusiveness, mutual learning, and mutual benefit. The Silk Road spirit has become a great heritage of human civilization."

Xi went through the origins of the ancient Silk Road with the dispatch by the Han Emperor of Zhang Qian, who opened the road to the West, launching a new era of collaboration between East and West, an exchange of goods and produce as well as an exchange of ideas and culture. China exported its four great inventions to the West (the compass, gunpowder, papermaking, and print-

Schiller Institute

Helga Zepp-LaRouche (lower right) and other participants on May 14, 2017, at the opening session of the Belt and Road Forum for International Cooperation.

ing), and received from the West the astronomy, medicine, and calendar of the Arabs. "History is our best teacher," Xi said. "The glory of the ancient silk routes shows that geographical distance is not insurmountable. If we take the first courageous step towards each other, we can embark on a path leading to friendship, shared development, peace, harmony, and a better future." Such is the paradigm he wished to build in this modern era as an alternative to the wars and conflicts that have marked the rule of "geopolitics." "From the historical perspective, humankind has reached an age of great progress, great transformation, and profound changes," Xi continued. "In this increasingly multi-polar, economically globalized, digitized, and culturally diversified world, the trend toward peace and development becomes stronger, and reform and innovation are gaining momentum. Never have we seen such close interdependence among countries as today, such fervent desire of people for a better life, and never have we had so many means to prevail over difficulties."

"In terms of reality, we find ourselves in a world fraught with challenges. Global growth requires new drivers, development needs to be more inclusive and balanced, and the gap between the rich and the poor needs to be narrowed. Hotspots in some regions are causing instability, and terrorism is rampant. Deficit in peace, development, and governance poses a daunting challenge to mankind. This is the issue that has always been on my mind," Xi said.

He then outlined some of the achievements of the first five years of the endeavor, noting how the Belt and Road dovetails with the individual development programs of the countries along the way. While he noted that the Belt and Road were a Chinese proposal, he underlined that the initiative itself is owned by all who participate and share in its benefits.

Xi then laid out five characteristics of the Belt and

China's President Xi Jinping delivers the keynote address at the Belt and Road Forum, May 14, 2017.

Road. First, it must become a road of peace. "We should foster a new type of international relations featuring win-win cooperation," Xi said, "and we should forge partnerships of dialogue with no confrontation and of friendship rather than alliance. All countries should respect each other's sovereignty, dignity, and territorial integrity, each other's development paths and social systems, and each other's core interests and major concerns," he said.

The Master Key

Second, it must become a road of prosperity. "Development holds the master key to solving all problems," Xi said. "In pursuing the Belt and Road Initiative, we should focus on the fundamental issue of development, release the growth potential of various countries and achieve economic integration and interconnected development and deliver benefits to all."

Third, it must be a road of opening up. "We should build an open platform of cooperation and uphold and grow an open world economy," he said. "We should jointly create an environment that will facilitate opening up and development, establish a fair, equitable and transparent system of international trade and investment rules, and boost the orderly flow of production factors, efficient resources allocation, and full market integration. We welcome efforts made by other countries to grow open economies based on their national conditions, participate in global governance and provide public goods. Together, we can build a broad community of shared interests."

And fourth, it must become a road of innovation. "We should spur the full integration of science and technology into industries and finance, improve the environment for innovation, and pool resources for innovation," Xi said. "We should create space and build workshops for young people of various countries to cultivate entrepreneurship in this age of the internet

President of Russia Vladimir Putin, left, and President of China Xi Jinping.

and Road Initiative to launch more projects to improve people's well-being. It will also provide emergency food aid worth RMB 2 billion to developing countries along the Belt and Road and make an additional contribution of US$1 billion to the Assistance Fund for South-South Cooperation.

China will also set up many new mechanisms to support the Belt and Road, Xi said, including a liaison office for the Forum's follow-up activities, along with the Research Center for Belt and Road Financial and Economic Development, the Facilitating Center for Building the Belt and Road, the Multilateral Development Financial Cooperation Center in cooperation with multilateral development banks, and an IMF-China Capacity Building Center.

President Putin's Historic Goal

The other speakers at the plenary following the Chinese President underlined their whole-hearted supported for President Xi's initiative. The first to follow the Chinese President, in a very important symbolism, was Russian President Vladimir Putin, the closest collaborator with President Xi among world leaders on the Belt and Road project. In his speech, Putin reiterated the complementarity of the Belt and Road project and Putin's own proposal for a Eurasian Economic Union (EAEU). "I believe," Putin said, "that by adding together the potential of all the integration formats like the EAEU, the OBOR (Belt and Road), the SCO (Shanghai Cooperation Organization) and the ASEAN (Association of Southeast Asian Nations), we can build the foundation for a larger Eurasian partnership. This is the approach that, we believe, should be applied to the agenda proposed today by the Peoples Republic of China. We would welcome the involvement of our European colleagues, which would make it truly concordant, balanced and all-encompassing, and will allow us to realise a unique opportunity to create a common cooperation framework from the Atlantic to the Pacific for the first time in history."

One after the other, government leaders and leaders of the international organizations spoke on behalf of the Belt and Road Initiative. New mechanisms were set up for financing and a Memorandum of Understanding

and help realize their dreams." In this regard, China, in the coming five years, will offer 2,500 short-term research visits to China for young foreign scientists, train 5,000 foreign scientists, engineers, and managers, and set up 50 joint laboratories.

Fifth, it must become a road connecting different civilizations. "In pursuing the Belt and Road Initiative," Xi said, "we should ensure that when it comes to different civilizations, exchange will replace estrangement, mutual learning will replace clashes, and coexistence will replace a sense of superiority. This will boost mutual understanding, mutual respect, and mutual trust among different countries."

To underline the Chinese commitment to the success of the initiative, Xi announced that China would commit an additional 100 billion RMB (about $14.5 billion) to the Silk Road Fund, and that the China Development Bank and the China Export-Import Bank would set up special lending schemes respectively worth 250 billion RMB and 130 billion RMB for Belt and Road projects on infrastructure, industrial capacity, and financing.

Xi announced that China will also provide assistance worth RMB 60 billion to developing countries and international organizations participating in the Belt

Xinhua

Leaders' Round Table Summit of the Belt and Road Forum, chaired by China President Xi Jing on May 15, 2017, the day after the opening session.

Roundtable at the conclusion of the conference, there were leaders of 30 countries as well as representatives of the UN, the World Bank and the IMF. They had reached, Xi said, a "broad consensus" in their exchange of view and had issued a joint communique.

Also attending the Forum was U.S delegation headed by Matthew Pottinger, head of the East Asia Bureau of the National Security Council and a Special Assistant to President Trump. Pottinger expressed support for U.S. companies becoming engaged in the Belt and Road Initiative and said that the U.S would set up an American Belt and Road Working Group, which would be a partnership between the U.S Embassy and U.S. companies and would serve, Pottinger said, "as a node for collaboration in the area."

was signed the multilateral development banks affirming their support for the Belt and Road Initiative.

In a press conference following the meeting, President Xi said that China had signed Belt and Road cooperation agreements with 68 countries. At the Leaders'

Belt and Road Initiative Sparking 'Profound Changes' in the World

May 15—Today Helga Zepp-LaRouche, chairwoman and founder of the Schiller Institutes, was one of the two guests on the China Global Television Network's prime-time, live interview show, "Dialogue with Yang Rui," following her participation in the Belt and Road Forum for International Cooperation, May 14-15 in Beijing. Yang's other guest was Dr. Su Ge, President of the China Institute of International Studies, the think tank of the Foreign Ministry of China.

This is EIR's transcription of the program, in which Dr. Su and Mrs. Zepp-LaRouche strongly agreed that, in his words, "profound changes ... tremendous changes" are already taking place in the world and that it is possible for people to give up their "dark glasses of the Cold War" and think differently. A video of the program is available here *and* here.

Yang Rui: Twenty-nine foreign leaders and more than 1,500 delegates from over 130 nations attended the Belt and Road Forum for International Cooperation in Beijing, from May 14 to 15. China's President, Xi Jinping, called the Belt and Road Initiative "the project of the century" in his keynote presentation at the opening ceremony. He also promised that China will create a new model of cooperation and mutual benefit in advancing the initiative. However, some critics are skeptical about China's goals for the initiative. To discuss the issues related to China's Belt and Road, I am pleased to be joined in the studio by Dr. Su Ge of the China Institute of International Studies and Helga Zepp-LaRouche, founder of the Schiller Institute. That's our topic. This is "Dialogue." I am Yang Rui.

'Project of the Century'

Yang Rui: What do you make of China's global initiative?

Helga Zepp-LaRouche: I think it's a very important strategic initiative because it's the only way in which you can solve all problems—regional, cooperation, underdevelopment, poverty. It's really a historic

CGTN/screen shot

Dr. Su Ge (left) and Helga Zepp-LaRouche (center) being interviewed by Yang Rui on his CGTN Dialogue show.

mission. I cannot see anything else, not from the United States—for sure, not from Europe—so I'm really optimistic. I think yesterday was a fantastic, historic moment.

Yang Rui: Yes. We see extensive media coverage about the Belt and Road Summit in Beijing. Dr. Su, among the following phrases to characterize the Belt and Road Initiative, which one do *you* prefer to choose: Global Ambition, World Leadership, or World Order, regarding the Belt and Road Initiative?

Su Ge: Well, probably some people say it is none of the above; some people would say it is all of the above. However, if you ask my opinion, I would say that the Belt and Road Initiative put forward by President Xi Jinping is a set of ideas and programs for peace, for prosperity, and for the future goodness of all countries and mankind, because now we are thinking of the whole human race, mankind, to have one destiny. We call it "shared destiny." And President Xi Jinping, in his speech, he said something,— well he is the head of a state. But sometimes he speaks like a historian, and also speaks like a philosopher.

Yang Rui: If not like the head of a big company. [Laughter.]

Su Ge: But he said, we have to find the general key to all existing problems in our world, in other words, development.

Yang Rui: [Cross-talk] … he wants to provide our own solution to some of the problems. But do you think China is ready?

Zepp-LaRouche: Oh, I think so. First of all, the Chinese economic miracle of the last 30 years has surprised the world. And now through the Belt and Road Initiative, China is offering to export that model of development to other countries. And if you look at the success of the Belt and Road Initiative in the last four years, it is absolutely breathtaking! And I am shocked— every day the Chinese government comes up with a new initiative which offers a solution to a problem. And it's just a very attractive idea. This is why so many countries want to be part of it.

It's much more attractive to have win-win cooperation in the context of the New Silk Road, than to be part of a military alliance that just gets countries into trouble. So this is why the whole center of power has completely shifted to Asia.

I am convinced that yesterday we experienced the formation of a new world economic order. It was a truly historic moment, and I think most of the participants in the Belt and Road Forum had that profound sense of being in the middle of making history for a new era for civilization. I am very excited because this is a phase-change of humankind. I think we are on the verge of…

Is the Belt and Road a Threat?

Yang Rui: No wonder President Xi Jinping calls the Belt and Road Initiative the "project of the century." Dr. Su, do you foresee peaceful coexistence between the Bretton Woods [system] and the Belt and Road Initiative? I notice that President Xi Jinping emphasized in his keynote presentation that the Belt and Road Initiative does not aim to replace some of the existing mechanisms and initiatives such as that of the Russian Federation; the Turkish government also comes up with its own ambitious plan. All politicians throughout the world have their own vision of what the future might hold for the global economy. Now what do you make of President Xi's pledge that the Belt and Road Initiative does not threaten to replace other, existing mechanisms?

Su Ge: Well that's a very good, an excellent question. You mentioned the Bretton Woods, and some people, indeed, compare the Belt and Road to the so-called Marshall Plan [launched] in 1947, after the Second World War. But actually, the Belt and Road Initiative is not like any of these, because as President Xi Jinping said, from a historical viewpoint, when you look at the pioneers who took part in the ancient Silk Road, people used camel caravans. They did not carry with them spears, cannons, or guns. It was not one civilization conquering the other, but one civilization brought with it good will, and goods of silk, tea, and other commodities. And [it was] for connectivity, for inter-connectivity, between and among peoples, among cultures and civilizations, in addition to business and trade.

Yang Rui: I am afraid the Indian government disagrees. They say, Hey, the Sino-Pakistani economic corridor will somehow go through the contentious, territorial area of India, the Kashmir, and therefore they refuse to get involved in the Belt and Road Initiative. The spokesperson of the Indian foreign ministry even protested against the idea of the economic corridor between China and its [India's] geopolitical rival, Pakistan. What do you think of the rivalry, the geopolitical rivalry that China wants to really keep a distance from?

Zepp-LaRouche: Well, first of all, India has always

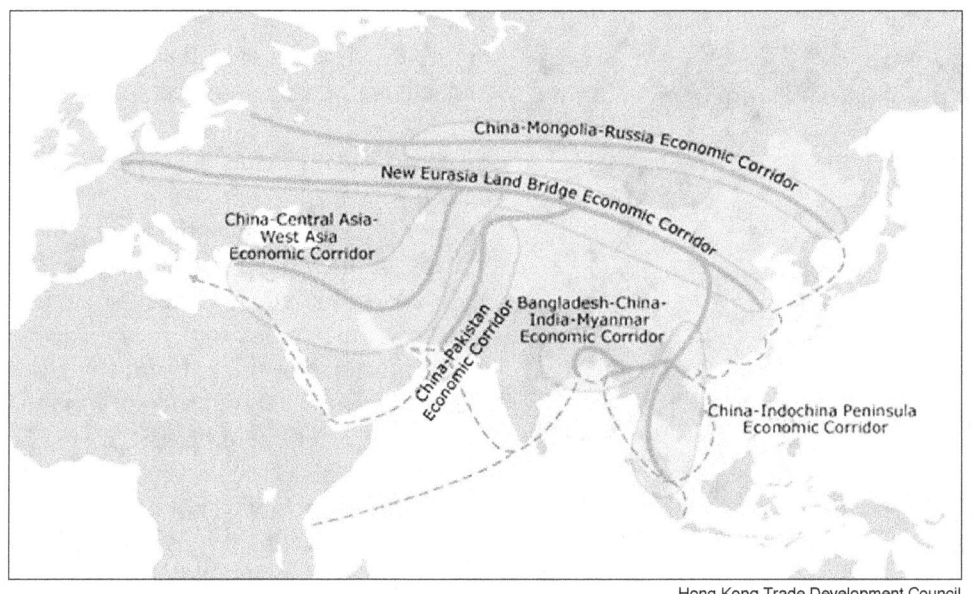

The Belt and Road Initiative: six economic corridors spanning Asia, Europe and Africa.

Hong Kong Trade Development Council

been the subcontinent, and therefore it has a long tradition of geopolitical thinking. But, I think this has been reinforced by British colonialism, and the British, and formerly the U.S. Administration before Trump, played on that. They played Pakistan as a source of state terrorism, trying to hype up sentiments in India to further this conflict.

But I think the opposite is true. Because of the British division of India into Pakistan, Bangladesh, and India, the only way this conflict can be overcome is by increasing the connectivity among all the countries: Nepal, Bangladesh, all these countries want to be integrated. And they call it "connectivity"; they don't call it the "Silk Road" and they don't call it "Belt and Road Initiative," because that's associated with China. But in substance, all of these countries urgently want more development like that of the Belt and Road Initiative.

The Eurasian Dumbbell

Yang Rui: Perhaps the Indian [word indistinct] is exactly based on a very sophisticated calculation about the BRICS Summit, which is to take place in China as well, this year, and therefore, they reject one, but agree to participate in the other. What do you make of the importance of the emerging markets, the shaping,— the vibrant markets of the developing countries? Some of the scholars from industrial nations say, Hey, why don't you invite the industrial nations to develop the countries, to get involved in this ambitious blueprint?

Su Ge: That's also a very nice question. When you look at the geography, the map of the Belt and Road ini-

tiatives, it is like something in sports, the dumbbell, with Europe as one end of the dumbbell and the Asia-Pacific region as the other. And the great landmass in between just serves as the handle. It just so happens that most of the countries of the area are developing countries. It is not that China chooses a group of countries to come as China's allies. China now has a foreign policy that China does not seek allies; we seek partners. It just so happened that all the countries in the handle between Europe and Asia, this Eurasia map, are developing countries. Of course, the developing countries need the development, they need prosperity, and the Belt and Road Initiative serves best their national interests. And we find a convergence of national interests. That's why these countries would like, *would love,* to jump on the boat.

Trump and the United States

And also, the Belt and Road initiatives are inclusive in nature. As President Xi Jinping said, it is open to all countries, to all. That's why you can see that the United States—well, maybe it is not along the traditional Silk Route—however, it decided to send a representative to the forum. So, as I . . .

Yang Rui: What's interesting is that both sides announced their joint projects—the list of projects agreed upon—simultaneously. Do you think something must have been discussed at the Mar-a-Lago summit in Florida, between Trump and President Xi Jinping? And that actually the announcement of this list of mega-projects between the two sides is an indispensable part of what has been agreed upon by the two heads of state?

Zepp-LaRouche: I think so, because President Trump has announced that he wants to have investment in $1 trillion worth of infrastructure in the next ten years. The American Society of Civil Engineers estimates that $4.5 trillion actually is required, and Chinese experts have said that the United States needs $8 trillion worth of infrastructure. Now China in the past years has shown a tremendous expertise in building fast trains and other infrastructure projects. China also has $1.4

CasonVids/youtube

President Trump meeting China President Xi Jinping at Mar-a-Lago, Florida, April 6, 2017.

trillion in U.S. Treasuries, which we have proposed be invested in an infrastructure bank or national bank in the United States, to make investments in the building of infrastructure.

Now that would be a total game-changer. And if China, in return, would invest in the Chinese market, which is growing because of its growing buying power, you could replace the competition between the United States and China through cooperation. And then they could join hands and have joint investments in third countries, like rebuilding the Middle East and developing Africa.

I think it's important that you're not just talking about infrastructure and economics. We are really talking about the new era of civilization, where you replace geopolitics with a completely new set of relations among countries. And if the United States and China could solve this,— you know, I have said many times that if President Trump would go for this, he could become one of the greatest Presidents in the history of the United States. Many of his critics don't think that is possible, but I am absolutely convinced that we are very close to it.

Yang Rui: Challenges lie ahead. One of them, I am afraid, is the alleged poor efficiency of the capital allocation. Many are very sceptical about the return on investment in developing countries in particular. What do you think are the risks?

Su Ge: It depends on how you look at it. In Chinese, we have a saying that when you look at a mountain when you are in front of it, it looks like a mountain range. But if you go to the side of it, it looks like all peaks. Perspectives matter!

Yang Rui: [Recites the saying in Chinese.]

Su Ge: For instance, if you just think like an ordinary businessman, in the Belt and Road Initiative, how much you put in and how much you want to gain back: well that's another thing. But then, if you regard this as a public product, a public good, then it will be a benefit, it will be shared by all of the countries, and then you will reap the gains, not only in terms of dollars and cents, but in connectivity, but people's understanding, marriage of civilizations, and then better lives for the future generations. And this will be a tremendous way to look at the Belt and Road.

China, Japan and Russia

Yang Rui: And in fact, overseas observers pointed out that President Xi Jinping was talking to two audiences at the opening ceremony. For the international audience, he promised to export our technology, our ideas about the Belt and Road Initiative; to re-establish the world order; and to reconsider the idea of globalization internally. He also promised to rejuvenate the nation, to tell a China story through the Belt and Road Initiative.

To the surprise of many who are very sceptical about the economic relationship between Japan and China— two arch-competitors, economically and geopolitically as well—the Japanese government decided to send a senior delegation, which was headed by the head of the ruling party, the LDP, Liberal Democratic Party. And this head of the delegation also handed over a letter from Prime Minister Shinzo Abe to the host of the Belt and Road Initiative summit. What do you think of the possibility that Japan will seize this opportunity to drastically improve not only the [words indistinct] ties, but also to enjoy the dividends of the Belt and Road Initiative, so that it will not be excluded from rebuilding the world economic order?

Zepp-LaRouche: I think it is very clear that Prime Minister Abe has the intention to do that. He sent the *de facto* number two of the LDP to the summit. I think it has to do with the change in perception, that the world is indeed changing.

Look at the rapprochement between Russia and Japan over the last period: Abe has the intention to have a peace treaty during his time in office. There were many visits by Abe to Russia, and vice versa, Putin visited Tokyo. Meanwhile, China has a very close relationship with Russia, and Trump has said he doesn't want to continue the offensive policies of the United States of interventions in foreign wars.

Then, the situation in the South China Sea has completely shifted; it's no longer such an important hot spot. I think we are on the verge of fixing the world according to completely new rules. It's really a time for people to rethink, and not to stick to old geopolitical schemes that were dominant in the Cold War, because we are on the verge of a completely new era of civilization, and I think what Abe did, reflects that.

Xinhua/Pang Xinglei

Japan Prime Minister Shinzo Abe (left), being greeted by China President Xi Jinping at the G-20 summit in Hangzhou, China on Sept. 5, 2016.

Scrap the Cold War Dark Glasses

Yang Rui: Ironically, the young leader of the D.P.R.K. test-fired a missile to coincide with the policy speech by President Xi Jinping at the opening ceremony. Yet the elected leader of the R.O.K., Mr. Moon, promised to reconsider the deployment of the THAAD, a missile shield program that may have paved the way for an apparent improvement in the bilateral relationship [between South and North Korea], which has been frayed seriously by the THAAD program. What do you think of, say, the R.O.K. delegation,— and in fact, a rumor went viral on the Internet that President Trump called for a boycott of the Belt and Road summit saying, "Hey, why did you invite the D.P.R.K. to attend the summit while the international society, through the UN Security Council, imposed yet another economic sanction?" I believe the new sanction is well underway. What do you think of the concerns, allegedly, a major concern, according to the international media?

Su Ge: There are two ways to look at the situation. One is to put your eyes as close as possible to the canvas. The other is to step back and look at the whole picture. I would say that the international situation is undergoing one of the most important, profound changes since the end of the Cold War. I agree with Zepp-LaRouche that there are tremendous changes already taking place. Maybe we are stepping into a new era, because the Cold War is over. If you still use the Cold War mentality, if you still look at world affairs in terms of zero-sum games, then things will appear different. I would say that you cast aside, people cast aside the dark glasses left over from the Cold War years.

Yang Rui: But I am afraid that those who are very skeptical about China's intent, may point out, citing President Bush, Jr., that bad behavior should not be rewarded. So this invitation for the D.P.R.K. delegation has been very controversial. I'd like to have your take on it.

Zepp-LaRouche: Well, I think there are some people who are thinking in terms of the old paradigm of geopolitics, and they can just not imagine that a country, especially a large country like China, would be motivated by Confucian ideas. And I have studied China for the better part of my life, and I have come to the conclusion that the present government, in particular, is not based on anything other than the Confucian idea of harmony among nations. And some people realize that. For example the Italian Prime Minister Gentiloni, at the Belt and Road Forum, gave a fantastic speech, in which he said ...

Yang Rui: Excuse me, but harmony would become a [words indistinct], if we do not respect some of the principles which have a lot to do with our national security. The nuclear program of the D.P.R.K. has indeed endangered the northern three provinces, Heilongjiang, Jilin, and Liaoning, if any nuclear fallout were to occur! That would be a major threat [crosstalk] to national security.

Zepp-LaRouche: But the new President of South Korea has basically said that he wants to go back to the Sunshine Policy of economic cooperation with the North. North Korea only has nuclear missiles because they were afraid they would have the same fate as Saddam Hussein or Qaddafi. And once that threat is taken away and we return to the Six Party Talks and the Sunshine Policy, and especially if this is in the context of the Belt and Road Initiative, I am absolutely confident that this problem will go away very shortly.

Let's Help North Korea Develop

Yang Rui: What do you think of China's efforts to leverage our limited influence on the D.P.R.K., by maintaining the links? Without the links, you will not be able to leverage the resources. By including the D.P.R.K., it showcases the readiness of the Chinese authorities to adopt an inclusive scheme. That is the essence of the Belt and Road Initiative, which aims to ensure an era of co-prosperity. And therefore, the D.P.R.K. should not be an island! What do you think of the intent of the Chinese government, which has drawn a lot of fire?

Su Ge: Allow me to quote from President Xi Jinping. He says that development is the key to all of these problems. What he is saying [relates to why] things are so complicated in Afghanistan. And some people wanted to solve the problems with a big stick, with military means. However, I doubt whether military means can eradicate the roots of radicalism. But eventually the key is development, and bringing up the people's consciousness through education and a better life.

For the D.P.R.K., the international community is carrying out sanctions by order of the UN Security Council. You have sanctions, you have tough measures, and you have to let them know that when you shut all of the doors, you have to leave one window open. That is the only way out. Through your reforms, through opening to the outside world, by construction, by letting the people go through the general road of market reforms. Then you can build up the economy. Then your people know that that is the only correct way out. The United States may say that,— some people are saying, "Let's get tougher!" Yes, people are carrying out the sanctions, Resolution 2270 and other measures, by the order through the UN Security Council. However, economic construction,— if finally, they embrace ideas of market reforms, I think that would be the correct way out.

Europe Will Join in the Belt and Road

Yang Rui: The last question is whether there's going to be a collision or a clash between Russia's brainchild of the Eurasian Economic Union, and the Belt and Road Initiative. Because there have been speculations by the media, saying, "Hey, Russia may show its great concern about China's interference with the internal affairs of its traditional backyard, Central Asia, through perhaps the role of the Shanghai Cooperation Organization." And therefore, they focus on whether there's going to be inconsistency and discrepancy between Russia's Economic Union and the Belt and Road Initiative. What's your take?

Zepp-LaRouche: You will be happy to hear that President Putin, who was the guest of honor at the Belt and Road Forum, already gave a press conference where he said that not only does Russia support the Belt and Road Initiative, but it will take an active role in promoting it.

And if you look at the number of leaders and countries that are now joining, you have a total change in the dynamic—Tsipras from Greece, the Serbian government, Hungary, the Czech Republic, Belarus, Italy, Spain, Portugal, and Switzerland—all of these countries have said they want to become hubs of the Belt and Road Initiative. So even if the German Economics Minister at the forum was not so friendly, let's say, I think Germany will be soon surrounded by countries that want to be part of it, and I think this will tilt the situation.

The former Prime Minister of France, Jean-Pierre Raffarin, gave a passionate speech about why France should be in it, and he was sent to the forum by the new President, Macron.

So I'm absolutely convinced that in half a year, the majority of the nations that are still reluctant, will recognize that it is in their best interest. Because, for example, Germany should have a fundamental interest in cooperating. German industry, the *Mittelstand*—medium-sized industry—is exactly the complementary kind of economic force that would perfectly work with China. And I think it will come around. I promise!

Yang Rui: Despite the success of Emmanuel Macron, the European Union is indeed in trouble. And President Trump's idea of prioritizing American interests, putting America first, may also isolate this country from the rest of the world. During this absence, China is said to be ready to assume the leadership. Is China ready? We'll keep this discussion open. Until next time, goodbye.

FBI's McCabe Attacks Anti-ISIS Virginia State Senator

The following interview with Virginia State Senator Richard Black took place on May 10, 2017. It was conducted by EIR's William Wertz. A full video of the interview may be found here*.*

William Wertz: My name is Will Wertz. I'm on the Editorial Board of *Executive Intelligence Review*, and I'm honored today to be able to interview Virginia Senator Dick Black. For those of you who may not be familiar with his history, Senator Black is a retired colonel. He flew 269 combat missions in Vietnam as a Marine pilot. He was wounded in fierce ground fighting of the First Marine Regiment, and later he became a career Judge Advocate General prosecutor and ran the Army's criminal law division at the Pentagon.

The reason we're doing this interview right now is that major developments have occurred, really in the last day or two, of which in a very real sense Senator Black is in the center. Just recently, President Trump fired Mr. James Comey, head of the FBI. He has been replaced with Andrew McCabe who is the Deputy Director of the FBI, and is now the Acting Director of the FBI, at least for a short period of time.

The point here is that Mr. McCabe's wife ran against Senator Black for state senator back in 2015, and this has become a big issue, particularly on the part of Sen. Chuck Grassley, who is chairman of the U.S. Senate Judiciary Committee, who has been very insistent about questioning what McCabe has been doing ever since that campaign, because of his involvement in the investigation of the Hillary Clinton e-mail controversy. Also, what has been his involvement in the investigation of the allega-

LPAC TV

Virginia State Senator Richard Black with William Wertz.

tions that the Trump campaign colluded with the Russians. There have also been suggestions that Mr. McCabe is a suspect in the leaking of certain classified information, including the transcript of the conversation between General Michael Flynn, and the Russian ambassador.

So let me ask Senator Black to comment on how he sees the importance of this?

Senator Richard Black: Yes, typically, I don't discuss any of my past opponents' issues. I've been in thirteen contested races, and typically I simply move on. But this is an issue of national significance, because it really deals with the fundamental integrity of the Department of Justice and the Federal Bureau of Investigation.

There are certain circumstances leading up to this that were very important. The local Democratic Committee had selected a candidate; they'd actually recruited someone to run against me in the 2015 election. The individual who was selected filed all of his paperwork, he obtained all of his petition signatures, he was totally filed. And then, word came down from Virginia Governor Terry McAuliffe, "he's out. We're putting in

Dr. Jill McCabe." It is my understanding that Governor McAuliffe, who was at the time under criminal investigation by the FBI, met with FBI Agent McCabe and with his wife to assist in the recruitment. And they did agree that she would run, and the word came down to the Loudoun County Democratic Party that the individual they had selected was not going to be the candidate; it was going to be this woman. There was not going to be a primary election, no contest. A decree had been issued by the governor, that this woman would be the candidate.

The individual, Thomas Mulrine, made a funny comment on his Facebook page after he had gotten everything ready to go, and he commented, "you hardly even knew me"! Which was true. He was a candidate, and then suddenly he was yanked in a very undemocratic process. Clearly, the governor wanted McCabe in this position, and it is my impression, just circumstantially, that he wanted him and he wanted his wife to be my opponent, not so much because of the wife as because of the fact that her husband was an up-and-comer in the FBI, and that Governor McAuliffe was under FBI investigation. He was extremely close, probably the closest individual there is, to Bill and Hillary Clinton, and Hillary Clinton was coming under investigation for the tremendous email scandal, one of the biggest scandals in recent history.

Eventually, she lost the race, but in the course of it, there were *floods* of money—we were stunned because we'd been through this so many times; this was our thirteenth election, and money was just pouring in. It was quite peculiar to us, and to the Republican Senate Caucus, and at one point Hillary Clinton came out to campaign for Jill McCabe in a *major* fundraiser—any time you have somebody of that stature who comes, she obviously is going to bring big money with her. And she was presently under investigation as I understand it. Now, we don't know the exact dates when FBI investigations start and finish, but all appearances are that both McAuliffe and Hillary Clinton were under criminal investigation by the FBI at the time.

Wertz: What I understand is that the meeting took place between Andrew McCabe, Jill McCabe and McAuliffe on March 2. That was the first time the *New York Times* reported on her email scandal; two days later they reported on the fact that she was using a private server. So this became public knowledge days

U.S. Federal Bureau of Investigation

Andrew McCabe, Deputy Director of the FBI.

before the meeting to recruit Jill McCabe.

Black: Clearly, you know, I've been involved in government ethics. I was on the General Staff at the Pentagon in the Office of the Judge Advocate General. Had this set of circumstances come to me, saying that someone was going to meet with two people who were under investigation, and the investigator was going to be the one who was going to be involved in the meetings, I would have said, "Absolutely, under *no* circumstances, may you do this! This is clearly forbidden by the Code of Federal Regulations." Now, that's my opinion. Others may have different opinions. People are able to manipulate the laws.

Wertz: What has been said is that Andrew McCabe consulted with people in the FBI with respect to his ethical obligations, and the FBI at some point put out a statement that he played no role, attended no events, and did not participate in fundraising or support of any kind. What's the actual story?

Black: We have photographs of him wearing a campaign tee-shirt. We know he was at public events, wearing a "Jill McCabe for Senate" tee-shirt, going around with her as she was shaking hands. So that was a very clear ethical violation, I think; not nearly of the significance of some of the others, but it was an ethical violation.

There was something else that happened. He was deeply involved in counter-terrorism activities, and he made an appearance at the local mosque, where historically, there had been a number of FBI investigations under way, and it was basically an outreach. That was how it was portrayed. It was an outreach to the community to better relations between the FBI and the Muslim community.

But the unusual thing about it was, first, on the website of the mosque, the Adams Center, it said that he was going to visit and that there would be no photography, and there would be no recordings permitted. It was to be a totally off-the-record discussion between him and a couple thousand people who were going to attend.

During those meetings, it was reported to me that he came right up to the line; he didn't ask for support for his wife, but he talked about how the FBI had to work very closely with the people in the mosque to ferret out potential terrorists and that sort of thing, things you would expect. But then he said, "I want to thank all of you for the tremendous support and the graciousness that you provided to my wife during her race for Senate in this district." I think any reasonable ethics attorney would have said, "Don't say that. That is crossing the line." It certainly has the appearance of impropriety.

Wertz: What Senator Grassley has more or less suggested is that there was a conflict of interest which Andrew McCabe had with respect to the investigation of Hillary Clinton's emails. The FBI was also investigating the Clinton Foundation as well as McAuliffe himself, personally, as you indicated. And he's raised other questions going forward. The suggestion is that McAuliffe recruited Jill McCabe, and there are certain indications that Andrew McCabe may have been interested in defeating you.

Now, let me just give our listeners an idea of who McCabe is, in terms of his background. He started out in the FBI in New York, working against Russian organized crime and Eurasian organized crime. Then he shifted to counter-terrorism. In 2006, McCabe was the unit chief for the FBI responsible for extraterritorial investigations of Sunni extremist targets. He later served as the assistant section chief of international terrorism,

www.grassley.senate.gov
Chuck Grassley, Senator from Iowa.

Operations Section 1, where he was responsible for FBI counter-terrorism investigations in the continental United States. In 2008, he was promoted to Assistant Special Agent in charge of Washington's field office counter-terrorism division. In September 2009, he was selected to serve as the first director of the High-value Interrogation group, which interrogates high-value terrorist suspects. In May 2011, he returned to the counter-terrorism division at FBI headquarters as Deputy Assistant Director to oversee international terrorism investigation programs. On Oct. 23, 2013, Comey named him Executive Assistant Director of the FBI's national security branch.

Now, in the period before Jill McCabe was recruited to run against you, you were very prominent—this was the period of at least 2013-2014—in opposing Obama's regime change policy, and his support for terrorists in many countries in the Middle East. Would you want to say something in terms of some of the activity that you were engaged in during that period?

Black: Yes, I studied the Syrian and Libyan situation very intensely, and I continue to do that to this day. What I determined through open-source intelligence was that the United States was very actively arming, training, and providing diplomatic cover for groups that were closely allied with al-Qaeda, the group which had brought down the Twin Towers and crashed planes into the Pentagon. I found this deeply disturbing.

I wrote a letter to President Bashar al-Assad in 2014, after his army had cleared the range of terrorists and he had rescued a great number of Christian communities—they were settled by the original Apostles, and many of them still spoke the language of Jesus, which is Aramaic. In the letter, I said, I want to thank the Syrian Arab Army for doing this, and particularly for rescuing the thirteen Catholic nuns who were held hostage. And I said, I want to thank you for the protection you've given the Christian community. I also said, I cannot explain to you why the United States, which lost 3,000 people on 9/11, has now turned and begun to support al-Qaeda, this very same organization that conducted this horrific attack on the United States.

SANA

Syrian pro-government forces and supporters of Syrian President Bashar al-Assad, hoisting their national flag in the western town of Yabrud, March 17, 2014.

and they had to listen to my hour-long lecture about Syria. Then they said, "Well, look, could you help us out?" And I said, "under the condition that I will have *no interaction whatsoever*, with terrorists, either ones who are on our watch list, or terrorist groups we are supporting," like Ahrar al-Sham, Jaysh al-Islam, Nour al-Zinki, al-Nusra—we were supporting them at the time. We were funnelling weapons to ISIS at the time. I said, I will not have *any* interaction with them.

Wertz: You also indicated at another time, they wanted you to get in touch with an organization in Syria.

Black: They did, and this was very interesting. They said: You know, if you got in touch with this group called al-Wafa, it might be that they would have some contacts. So, I said, "well, we'll certainly look at that." Now, we're very cautious; we will never be photographed with a terrorist, we will never do a telephone conference with a terrorist, anyone listed on the State Department list. The State Department maintains a list of terrorist organizations. So we took al-Wafa, we ran it against the list, and we found that Executive Order 13224 listed al-Wafa as a terrorist organization. I went back to the FBI, and I said, "I assume that you are not asking me to contact this organization; regardless of its efficacy, I have no legal authority to communicate with *any* organization officially designated as one that supports terrorism." And I said, "I have prepared a final draft letter," one that we had discussed, that they had asked for. But before I contact al-Wafa, I said, "I want written confirmation from the FBI, not from the State Department, which was *deeply* involved in supplying terrorist forces in Jordan, Qatar, Saudi Arabia and Turkey, who were being trained to invade Syria, in clear violation of international law.

This was really the first break in the wall. No one had dared to break the wall of government censorship that concealed what the United States was doing in Syria, and the fact that we were arming, training, and supporting al-Qaeda-linked terrorists. The letter created a worldwide firestorm—I mean, literally every major newspaper across the world covered that particular letter. It certainly put me on the cover pages. Around a similar time, I was designated an "enemy of ISIS." There were three Americans who were designated: Rick Santorum was one of the others. And so, I had made enemies of ISIS, and enemies of the Administration at the same time.

Wertz: What you indicated to me was that after this letter was published on President Assad's Facebook page, and you got all of this coverage internationally, the FBI came into contact with you.

Black: I had a very interesting exchange: The FBI contacted me and asked if I would help them to rescue some American journalists, who had been picked up by the Syrian authorities, and I said, "Absolutely, I will do it." But, I said, "On one condition; I will not provide *any* assistance to anyone committing terrorist acts against the Syrian government, or terrorists generally." They said, fine, these people are not in that category. So they flew two FBI agents, I forget whether it was from Florida or Georgia, but they came up and there were two locals—so I had four FBI agents who met with me,

I said, if you can give me the assurance, from the FBI, I want *you* to be on the dime if there is something wrong. They came back, and they did give me assurance that this al-Wafa group was a different one with a similar name, so I reported that in writing.

But the whole thing is so fishy. I said, "Why can't you get me the names?" I said, "We've got a war going on, we've got a very large prison system"—because the Syrians actually take captives, whereas the terrorists simply beheaded everyone that they caught. So I said, we've got a lot of captives; I can track them down and I can help you. But they said, "No, the State Department won't let us do that." It was a very mysterious approach.

So I did contact the Syrian government, and they said they would help, but of course, obviously there was little they could do without names. Later on, several months later, they contacted me again, and they said, "We really would like you to get involved in trying to recover these people," but by then I was fed up, and I said: "Look, either you give me names or you stop contacting me!" I said, "I will not be involved in contacting terrorists. If you want to do it, you do it. I will not contact terrorists under any circumstances," and at that point they broke contact. They realized, whatever they were trying to get out of me, they weren't getting it from me.

DoD photo by Erin Kirk-Cuomo
Egyptian President Abdel Fattah el-Sisi.

Wertz: The interesting thing here is that when you say two of the four FBI agents were local, well "local" in northern Virginia is the Washington, D.C. field office, which was run by Andrew McCabe, who as I just indicated, his entire background is counter-terrorism, including Sunni terrorists.

Black: Yeah, and the terrorists we are talking about, the ones that the U.S. is supporting and arming, these are all Sunni terrorist organizations. There are many good Sunnis in Syria, but we're importing Sunnis from around the world and we're training them. The Sunnis make up al-Qaeda, al Nusra, Jaish al-Islam, Ahrar al-Sham, all of these people. They're pouring over the Turkish border, they're pouring over the Jordanian border, and they're being trained by CIA organizations under an operation code-named "Timber Sycamore." That's been highly classified; it's been disclosed, so now it's reasonable to disclose

the name, Timber Sycamore.

Wertz: From what I understand, the President of Egypt is also Sunni, and you earlier wrote a letter to him, encouraging him to run for President of Egypt, after the Muslim Brotherhood, which Obama and Hillary Clinton had supported, had been overthrown by the Egyptian people.

Black: Yes. I wrote a letter to President [Abdel Fattah] el-Sisi, and it was clear he was the one to lead the country. We had a very nice exchange of communications. He wrote back, a letter that I actually have framed on my wall, and he was elected. I was the first American to break this wall of silence. I'm going to tell you, there is a very disturbing force that operates in the U.S. Congress that censors information. There are those who simply believe whatever they're told by the State Department, and there are those who know the truth and who live in terror, and will not disclose anything that they know the State Department does not want disclosed.

So I was the first American official to stand for President el-Sisi, who really has become one of the great leaders of the world and one of our great allies.

Wertz: Exactly. So, if you look at this, you opposed Obama's policy of regime change, which was also backed by the British, the French, the former colonial powers in Syria. What we're talking about here is that your letter to Assad was posted on his website—this was back on May 28, 2014. Soon after that you get visitations from the FBI, in a very fishy operation, and at least two of those agents are coming from the Washington, D.C. field office which is run by Andrew McCabe. This is ten months before his wife is recruited, in a meeting that he attends, with [then Virginia Gov. Terry] McAuliffe, to run against you.

Whereas some have looked at this from the standpoint merely of—there was sort of an agreement that she was backed to run, involving a conflict of interest in which Andrew McCabe ends up involved in various cases involving Hillary Clinton, the Democratic Party and eventually against Donald Trump; but the point that

I would make is that you had identified yourself as an opponent to the policy which was being carried out by the Obama administration and by the FBI, the CIA and the State Department in terms of regime change and the promotion of terrorists.

Black: Well, and worldwide, I was the first one to break the wall of silence. Since then, we have Rep. Tulsi Gabbard, we have Sen. Rand Paul, we have several who have come out and who have taken a stand; our own Virginia Rep. Tom Garrett. But up until this time there was total censorship. It was wartime censorship; it was censorship that was the equivalent of what we saw in the Second World War, when we were at war. We're not at war, and yet, we have this same type of censorship going on. I think there was a feeling that this individual, this Senator from Virginia, has to be just beaten into dust as an example to the world that if you dare to stand up and to tell the truth about what we're doing in Syria, and in other countries, then you're going to be crushed, your life is going to be destroyed. ...

Wertz: On June 10, 2016 you endorsed Donald Trump for President.
Black: Yes.

Wertz: I believe that Trump's willingness to break from the regime change policy was a major factor in that.
Black: It really was. I gave the major speech for him, leading up to his presentation in Richmond, Virginia right after the Republican National Convention; and I gave the major speech for him in Leesburg, Virginia, the night before Election Day, when he made a swing through, and we have that one recorded. Very, very strongly pro-Trump. I wanted to see him win, and I wanted him to win because I very much wanted to see Michael Flynn as the National Security Advisor; he knew where all the skeletons are buried. He genuinely desired to lessen tensions with Russia and also to move away from this business, this bloody business of regime change, of slaughtering people in countries all over the Middle East.

Believe me, I want to say: I'm not an anti-war activist. My radiomen were killed right beside me, and I was wounded trying to rescue a Marine outpost. When I was flying, my aircraft was hit four times by enemy ground fire. I have probably seen as much bitter combat as anybody has seen in a generation. So I'm not afraid to put my life on the line for my country, but at the same time, as a Marine, we used to sing the Marine Corps Hymn,

and it says, "to keep our honor clean..." And our honor is *not clean* in Syria; it was not clean in Libya, and I'm determined to do everything in my power to turn it around so that we can once again have a foreign policy that we're proud of and that serves the interests of the American people.

Wertz: In that same time period when you endorsed now President Trump, there were two interventions into the U.S. political scene by British intelligence. The first was a dossier that was compiled by an MI6 British intelligence officer, Christopher Steele, and the indications are that he actually worked on this dossier after being paid by the Clinton campaign, Hillary Clinton's campaign, to present this dossier. One of the issues that Senator Grassley has raised is—this was reported in the *Washington Post*—the FBI was prepared to pay Christopher Steele to continue his research to try to prove that Trump was somehow working with the Russians.

Black: Amazing that the FBI was involved in paying for opposition research! Now, I've done a little opposition research: You know, we paid companies, and of course it's been done on us, endlessly. But, I've read a little bit about *that* dossier, and if I paid someone and he gave me *that*, I would be so furious, because it is so transparently fallacious. It's just ridiculous! You know, unbelievable the things that he says. It has no air of credibility in my view, from my experience, and I've seen a lot of this stuff before. I think it was a total creation.

Wertz: The second intervention, which occurred also in the summer of 2016—and this was covered in an article in the *Guardian*—the head of GCHQ, the British equivalent of the NSA, Robert Hannigan, passed material to CIA chief John Brennan, again trying to claim that Trump or his associates were in some way working with the Russians. The irony here is that what's being claimed, is that the Russians are interfering in U.S. elections; and yet what we have is MI6 and GCHQ directly intervening, not just in the elections, but in the *aftermath* of the elections, to try to prevent Trump, as the President of the United States, from carrying out his policies. Particularly with respect to reversing everything that Obama had done in terms of the hostility to Russia, joining in the united front to fight today's equivalent of fascism, terrorism.

And one of the questions which [Senator] Grassley asks in respect to McCabe, he says: "Was McCabe involved in approving or establishing the FBI's reported arrangement with Mr. Steele? Or, did Mr. McCabe

New York Daily News/youtube

Christopher Steele

vouch for, or otherwise rely on the politically funded dossier in the course of the investigation? Simply put, the American people should know if the FBI's second in command relied on Democrat-funded opposition research to justify an investigation of the Republican Presidential campaign."

Black: That's a pretty stunning statement. Senator Grassley is probably one of the most highly respected members of the Senate. From everything he's done, everything I've seen, he has been neutral, he has been honest, he has been relatively non-partisan. He wants a good, clean justice system—so for him to be so aggressive about the potential misconduct by Andrew McCabe, I think, speaks volumes.

Wertz: Now, Sen. Chuck Grassley raises a further point, and these questions are included in a letter which he wrote, I believe on May 2, to Mr. Rod Rosenstein, who is the current Deputy Attorney General under Sessions. This is the same Rosenstein who recommended that Comey be fired; so all of these issues were raised by Grassley in a letter to Rosenstein, approximately a week ago.

The final point that Grassley raises is this, to Rosenstein: "What steps do you plan to take to ensure that the apparent leaks of classified information related to contacts between Trump associates and Russians are fully and impartially investigated, given that several senior FBI officials, including Mr. McCabe, are potential suspects with access to the leaked information?"

And I would also just mention that the *Daily Beast* reports the following: "Administration sources said McCabe had been eyed as a possible leaker of tran-

scripts of calls between Flynn and Russia's Ambassador to Washington. The transcripts show them discussing U.S. sanctions against the country and led to Flynn's firing from the White House in February."

Black: Well, McCabe—there is sort of an air of corruption, and it surrounds the senior leadership of the FBI. I read the letter by the Chairman of the Judiciary [Committee] Chuck Grassley. When he wrote it to Rosenstein, he said, essentially, now you are in this position, you need to clean this place up. You need to get it in order. And I think Rosenstein said, you know what, we're going to get it in order. We're going to start from the top. We're going to get Director Comey out; he's been scathingly criticized by both Democrats and Republicans. He clearly has exceeded his mandate, which is to investigate crimes. He has gone out and decided who is going to be prosecuted, who is not going to be prosecuted, which is the purview of the Department of Justice. So he was acting highly inappropriately.

And then McCabe, as the number two, has such a volume of ethical improprieties swirling around him, allegations of this and that. What you mentioned about his long experience in counterintelligence, beginning focused on the Sunni terrorist organizations, is very disturbing. You wonder if he has not been, to some degree, co-opted, perhaps by his personal ambition or whatever, and whether that played into his desire to see me brought down one way or the other.

Wertz: On Oct. 24, 2016, you issued a statement, "FBI Deputy Director Andrew McCabe Must Resign for Conflicts of Interest in the Hillary Clinton Email Scandal." The same article in the *Daily Beast* which I mentioned just a few minutes ago, says that McCabe, who is now Acting FBI Director, may not remain in that position long: "But even that leadership change could be short lived. Sources say McCabe will likely resign or be fired, though a well-wired federal law enforcement source told the *Daily Beast* that, given current national security threats, it's unlikely that would happen for the next few weeks." So, this is sort of a rhetorical question—what do you think will happen with Mr. McCabe? What do you think, really, the chances are of President Trump being able to move forward with the policy orientation which was the reason you supported him in the first place?

Black: Well, those are two different questions. I do believe that Andrew McCabe is going to leave shortly. I think there will be new and improved leadership in the Federal Bureau of Investigation. Up until now, before

Defense Intelligence Agency

Lt. Gen. Michael Flynn

Trump, DOJ and FBI really had sort of an aura of corruption surrounding them at the very highest levels. I think to some extent Trump can chalk this up as beginning to drain the swamp. Now that's one issue.

The other issue, however, is whether we are moving to change our policy of regime change, which has been very bloodthirsty; it's cost millions of lives and untold treasure of the United States. I'm troubled by the fact that Michael Flynn was eliminated, principally because, after Trump was elected, Michael Flynn went into action and began to communicate with world leaders. Frankly, if I had been the President-elect, and my National Security Advisor had gone off to Tahiti to sip cocktails, I'd have fired him. I would have expected that he would *immediately* begin communicating with top leaders, because you've got to be able to hit the ground running. I think one of the terrible mistakes that has been made was firing Michael Flynn. Michael Flynn wanted to reorient us in a very positive direction.

You need to realize that, back when I was serving in Germany in the Cold War, I was responsible for North Africa and the Middle East, and at the time Americans could travel *anywhere*, and people loved them.

Today, people fear them; people sometimes hate them, at least the government. They are very leery of the American government. So we have lost so much prestige in the Middle East and throughout the world, through our endless intermeddling in other governments.

I think Michael Flynn realized this. Some of the people he was with realized it; [Trump's Deputy National Security Advisor] K.T. McFarland, she was taken out. It remains to be seen.

I think Donald Trump knows, I think he understands, the disastrous direction where we were headed. Whether he can turn around this vast neo-con organization—it's not just American, it really expands; it covers the European Union, Great Britain, the Arab [Gulf] Cooperation Council, a tremendous portion of the wealthy Western world and the Middle East—whether he can get control of that, I don't know.

He must end the war in Syria, and the Syrian government must remain intact, because there are two choices: Either President Assad and the Syrian government and the Syrian army will retain control, or al-Qaeda, the group that brought down the Twin Towers and its allies, will gain control. There are two forces in this war, *it's as clear as that*. Until we recognize this, and stop playing games and trying to confuse people, then we run the risk of revitalizing a much larger Caliphate than ISIS ever formed. This will become not only a danger to the Middle East, it will become a danger to Israel; Jordan and Lebanon will fall almost immediately, and it will begin an Islamic drive on Europe, and I believe that this time Europe will fall.

Syria is the center of gravity in the war on terror. If we lose Syria, *because of our own actions*, then we lose the war on terror, with unforeseeable consequences, but very bad consequences.

Wertz: Well, I just want to thank you, for the courage that you have demonstrated. And for the fact that, as you pointed to, you've stood out, you broke the silence, other people are beginning to do so. I think really the issue of whether we succeed is up to the American population. Do they finally understand the need to ensure that we have a government by the consent of the governed, and do they take responsibility for the direction of the country?

Black: Thank you very much for doing this. Ultimately we will find out in the coming years whether the American people run this country or whether there will be global oligarchs who make decisions in Davos, Switzerland, and they control the entire globe. We must break forth; we must re-establish American sovereignty. And we must act to end the support for terrorists, so that we can win the war on terror. Thank you so much.

Wertz: Thank you.

In Honor of Gen. Harold Bedoya And His Mission

by Gretchen and Dennis Small

May 9—Colombian patriot General Harold Bedoya passed away on May 2 at the age of 78, after a battle with cancer. In his distinguished career, he served as Commander of Colombia's Army and Armed Forces, as Defense Minister, ran twice for president, and fought to rally his fellow citizens to drive the drug trade and all its instruments out of his beloved Colombia, until the very end of his life. Bedoya always saw himself, as he said, as being "on active duty for the nation." He did so knowing that he was acting on behalf of humanity as a whole.

Gen. Harold Bedoya
EIRNA

Informed of Bedoya's passing, American statesman Lyndon LaRouche asked that his name be added to those remembering Gen. Bedoya with respect and appreciation, "for my loyalty to that mission which he represented."

In February 2003, LaRouche and Gen. Bedoya held a joint seminar in Washington, D.C., on the subject of "The War on Drugs and the Defense of the Sovereign Nation-State." In their remarks, both addressed the quality of leadership required to pull the world out of crisis. "The issue here, that General Bedoya is most actively representing, is a crucial one for us all," LaRouche told the gathering. "The drug-pushing operation is the enemy of humanity. Kill it, and save the people. And wherever we find someone in a nation, who is capable and willing to stand up and defend those principles, we must work with them. We must find them as representative of what we hope to build on this planet, a community of principle among sovereign nation-states, as the future permanent guarantor of a condition of peace on this planet, from which standpoint humanity can go forward, to become finally, what we have not yet achieved: to become truly the human beings we were made to be."[1]

Bedoya, for his part, stated that "the crises that we are facing today throughout the world, but most especially here in the Americas, require leaders, great leaders, who understand the issues, and who are willing to assume responsibility, and fight, come what may, without becoming intimidated by lies and slanders, by tragedies, by lack of means or resources. Because, above and beyond man lies the strength of a God, Who shall lead us to the promised land of freedom, democracy, and all of that for which we have been born, and for which we shall die.

"So, I'm not too concerned about living through moments of difficulty," Bedoya continued, "because it is precisely at such moments of crisis that people are reborn, solutions emerge, and leaders such as Lyndon LaRouche appear, to tell the world to wake up, to tell Americans to please not be indifferent to this tragedy that we are facing throughout the Americas and the world."[2]

Gen. Harold Bedoya was just such a leader among men. At a time when most around him, in Colombia and across the Americas, were taking the easy way out and succumbing to the devastating paradigm shift that increasingly tolerated legalized drug consumption and production, Bedoya took personal responsibility to free Colombia from the murderous narcoterrorism which the Colombian people have suffered for decades, whether that terror came from the Medellin or Cali car-

---

1. "The War on Drugs and the Fight for National Sovereignty," *EIR*, March 24, 2000.
2. Ibid.

tels or from the FARC cartel today. He stood up against every Colombian government which capitulated to the "lead or money" terror—accept our bribery or be killed—waged against the nation by the Wall Street and the City of London financial powers which deploy the drug cartels.

Bedoya said "no." He refused to accept that Colombia cut a deal with the drug trade and become a narco-state. Not when Presidents Ernesto Samper Pizano (1994-1998) and Andres Pastrana (1998-2002) handed enormous swaths of territory (and the Colombians within that territory) over to the FARC cocaine cartel terrorists, and not when today's British project, President Juan Manuel Santos, sought to co-govern with the FARC and legalize the production, trafficking, and consumption of narcotics first in Colombia, and then worldwide.

Bedoya's unbending opposition to any "peace" with the drug trade was premised on moral grounds; he understood the drug trade to be "a crime against humanity." In an interview with *Executive Intelligence Review* in 1998, Bedoya called the idea of legalizing drugs "absurd."

"We have to fight the drug-trafficking mafias, so that not only will they not continue to produce drugs, but so that they cannot continue to cause the horrendous damage to which the youth and the entire world are being subjected through drugs. I believe that what we have to do here, rather than legalize drugs—it makes no ethical sense to do this—is to make drug-trafficking a crime against humanity, and we should try the drug mafias in international courts, as befits any civilized society in the world."[3]

When President Samper Pizano forced Gen. Bedoya into retirement in July 1997 as demanded by the FARC and its ELN guerrilla cousins, Bedoya did not waste a moment. Within a month, he was organizing a campaign for President based on a new political movement, Fuerza Colombia, which he mobilized on the principle that Colombia had a right to develop and prosper, free of drugs and narcoterrorism. As he campaigned across the nation (which he knew like the back of his hand from his travels to nearly every corner and village during years of active military service), he told his fellow Colombians: "Don't try to sell me the story, that in order to achieve peace, we have to hand over pieces of our country to criminals, to terrorists... All is not lost."[4]

An International Ambassador To Save Colombia

Knowing that "what we military men call the 'theater of operations' of the mafia and the drug trade is worldwide,"[5] Bedoya took his campaign against the drug menace to the rest of the Americas. Colombia did not have the resources to win a war against the international drug trade alone. Over the next few years, he traveled to the United States, Argentina, Brazil, Uruguay, and Peru organizing for these and other nations "to forge an alliance to do battle against the drug trade."[6] Each nation involved must commit to crushing the facet of the drug trade which afflicts it, be it crops, precursor chemicals, money, transport, weapons supply, or consumption, he said.

He argued that with such an alliance, the drug trade could be wiped out in two years—provided it was accompanied by economic development. Colombia has been reduced "to ashes" economically by the drug trade, "narcotized," no longer producing its own food, Bedoya said. He proposed a "Marshall Plan" approach, in which the great world powers would collaborate in the reconstruction of Colombia. With international contributions of capital, technology, and trade—and without International Monetary Fund conditionalities, he insisted—Colombia could establish development poles in the regions devastated by the drug trade, in which the State would initiate a civil-military mobilization, and deploy its military engineers to help build schools and large infrastructure projects: highways, bridges, railways, airports, canals, sea and river ports, thus "putting the land to work once again to grow food instead of drugs, recovering the jungle that was burned or slashed to produce coca."[7]

Turning the Tide in the United States

Everywhere he went, Bedoya fearlessly took on Wall Street and the U.S. State Department, by name, for backing the drug mafias. In June 1999, Madeleine Albright's State Department had organized the visit of the head of the New York Stock Exchange, Richard Grasso,

---

3. "Colombia and the U.S. Can Jointly Defeat Narco-Terrorism." Interview by Dennis Small in *EIR*, July 3, 1998.
4. "Gen. Bedoya: To Win, Mobilize the Nation," *EIR*, May 8, 1998.

5. "General Bedoya: In Two Years, We Can Get Rid of the Drug Trade." Speech given at an *EIR* seminar on "The Peruvian and Colombian Peace Processes," in Bogota, Colombia on July 23, 1998. Translated and published in *EIR*, August 7, 1998.
6. Address to the Argentine Council on Foreign Relations (CARI) on August 10, 1999. Translated and published in *Executive Intelligence Review*, August 27, 1999.
7. "General Bedoya: In Two Years, We Can Get Rid of the Drug Trade." See note 5.

ANCOL/Fernando Ruiz

The infamous "Grasso Abrazzo": New York Stock Exchange president Richard Grasso embraces Colombian drug kingpin Raúl Reyes, at his jungle hideout.

to the FARC-controlled Caguan demilitarized zone. Upon his return, Grasso announced, on a conference call with the press, that in his view the FARC understood capital markets very well, and he hoped that, soon, he could escort Comandante Tirofijo—the head of the FARC cocaine cartel—down the hallways of the New York Stock Exchange to discuss "mutual investments." That same month, the IMF publicly ordered the Colombian government to include drug production figures in its GDP calculations, treating drugs as just another input into the Colombian economy.

In early September 1999, Gen. Bedoya made an intervention in Washington, D.C. which proved decisive. The Wall Street faction in the State Department was pressing hard for Colombia to consummate the deal with the FARC signaled by the Grasso visit. Anti-Drug Czar Gen. Barry McCaffrey and other patriots, in and out of government, opposed that immoral policy as leading to a strategic disaster.

Gen. Bedoya came to Washington in the middle of this fight, on a trip organized by LaRouche's *EIR* magazine. For seven days, from 7 a.m. to midnight, Bedoya held private meetings with more than a dozen Congressional and Senate offices, including nine Representatives and three Senators personally; with high-level officials at the State Department; and with U.S. military officers, urging the United States to join Colombia in a total battle against narcoterrorism and the drug trade. He addressed a special *EIR* seminar organized for dip-

lomats from around the world; gave numerous press interviews, including a very well attended briefing at the National Press Club; addressed 1,000 American citizens from across the U.S. at the semi-annual Schiller Institute conference; and he spoke to a meeting with the Colombian community.

In every speech, seminar or personal meeting he had, as he had in his earlier travels in South America, Bedoya held up or spoke about the infamous "Grasso Abrazo" picture of Stock Exchange head Grasso hugging Comandante Raúl Reyes, the head of FARC finances, during his visit to the Caguan. Bedoya asked, as he had in every stop in his prior tour in South America: What is Colombia supposed to conclude from such a visit? "It would be very good if the government of the United States were to interrogate those gentlemen, who landed on the same airstrips from which the drugs which so concern U.S. authorities are exported."[8]

Bedoya depicted vividly for his American audience the horrors which Grasso's narcoterrorist allies had brought, such as some 4,000 children, age 10-16, kidnapped from their families to become cannon fodder for the FARC forces, and the estimated 1,500 adult Colombians kidnapped and held in FARC camps. His detailed map briefings made clear the strategic implications of just how much of Colombia's territory was already in the hands of the narcoterrorists.

Bedoya called upon the United States to understand that Colombia's fight is its fight, to find the political will to support Colombia and its neighbors in an all-out political-military war against narcoterrorism, and to provide the kind of economic development needed for victory. His message was simple: "This is not a Colombian mafia; it is an international mafia. United, we can finish them off."[9]

He specified the assistance that Colombia needed: modern military weaponry and equipment, with train-

---

8. "Colombia's Bedoya Proposes South American Alliance vs. Narco-Terrorism," *Executive Intelligence Review,* August 27, 1999.

9. "General Bedoya Proposes War on Narco-Terrorism: 'United, We Can Finish Them Off,'" Sept. 10, 1999 interview with United States Information Agency's Foro Interamericano television program, transcribed, translated and published by *Executive Intelligence Review,* Oct. 1, 1999.

ing for their efficient use, satellite and other intelligence, and Marshall Plan-style economic aid for reconstruction. Under no circumstances, he insisted, does that mean foreign troops entering Colombian territory, repeating to everyone on this point: "no, no, no, no."

Bedoya laid out his message for the record in an interview with the United States Information Agency's Foro Interamericano [Inter-American Forum] television program, a message which is as urgent today as it was then:

"The U.S. does not have to send troops to Colombia. Providing technical and logistical aid is the most important, and don't send out signals that coca is good, as one Wall Street faction did—Mr. Richard Grasso practically walked into the laboratories to negotiate with Wall Street's money. No one can fathom what Wall Street and the International Monetary Fund are doing, demanding that Colombia include drug trade revenues as part of GDP! That makes us a narco-democracy, in which drugs here, and in the world, are practically being legalized....

"If the United States does not do what it should do, it will suffer the consequences. So the United States must make a decision very soon. Every minute, every day, every second that passes, means that the problem will be solved with more [drug] money, more deaths, more terrorism, and, of course, more drug-trafficking....

"The peace process exists because the U.S. government backs it. That is, the U.S. has that responsibility, and that's why its so important that the United States rectify and correct its mistake. ... Colombia is dying. ... A rectification in time could save Colombia and America."[10]

Several years later, qualified U.S. military sources told *EIR* that Gen. Bedoya's trip had tipped the balance in the fight in Washington against Wall Street's legalization-through-peace faction. The decision was made to aid Colombia through Plan Colombia instead. Plan Colombia did not meet the criteria required for victory which Bedoya had specified, but it did establish the principle that the U.S. must support Colombia in its

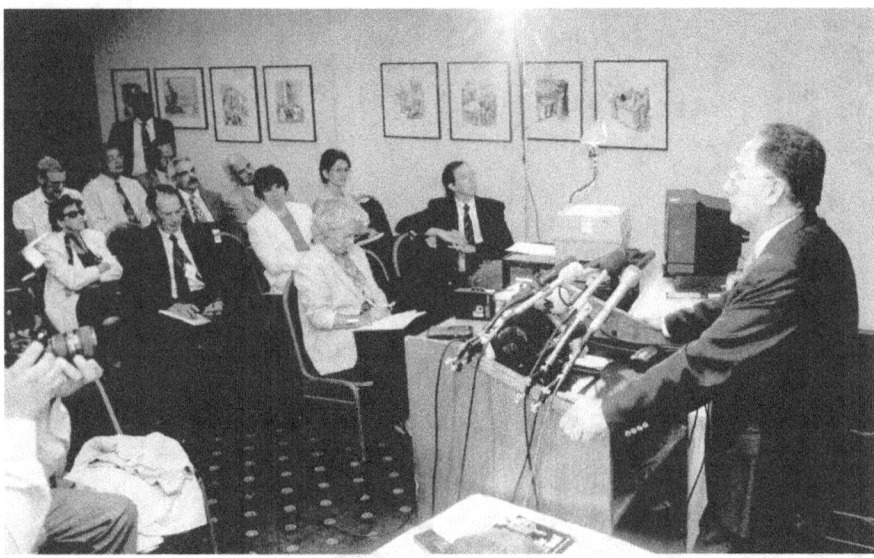
EIRNS/Stuart Lewis

Harold Bedoya holding a news conference: "Stop narco-terrorism in Colombia: How the U.S. and Colombia can collaborate to defeat the narco-terrorists who are dismembering that South American nation," Washington, D.C., Sept. 7, 1999.

fight against drugs and narcoterrorists. The basis was laid for the collaboration, albeit more limited than that required, which was critical to Colombia's military campaign under President Alvaro Uribe Velez (2002-2010) which freed major sections of Colombia's territory and people from the FARC cartel's control, lowering drug production significantly in the process.

A People's General

As a true military leader, Bedoya understood that "wars without a valid moral purpose are a total failure. The fundamental thing," he argued, "is to determine if there exists a higher-order moral purpose that justifies the war, and also if there is the will to win and to impose a just, and therefore lasting peace." He went directly to the Colombian people because he understood that "wars are not won by powers; wars are won by the people. The only ones capable of resolving an internal problem are the people themselves."[11]

His entire life, Gen. Harold Bedoya stood his ground against the deadly tide of the international drug trade, and sought to bring about a peace fit for human beings. For that, the nation of Colombia, and an entire generation of American youth, owe him a debt of gratitude.

---

11. "Bedoya on the 'New NATO' and a Marshall Plan for Colombia." Speech given by Gen. Bedoya to the May 6, 1999 *EIR* conference: "In the Face of the Financial Collapse, the New NATO Threatens the World," translated and published by *Executive Intelligence Review,* June 4, 1999.

---

10. Ibid.

Cheminade: The Challenge And the Work Starts Now!

EIR *editor Tony Papert interviewed Lyndon La-Rouche's friend, former French Presidential candidate Jacques Cheminade, on May 15, 2017.*

EIR: The great summit on the Belt and Road Initiative is still going on in Beijing as we're speaking, and I understand that France is represented by former Prime Minister Jean-Pierre Raffarin, currently a Senator. What can you say about what should be France's role in the great tasks of the future—the World Land-Bridge or the Belt and Road Initiative, and the exploration of the Solar system and beyond?

Jacques Cheminade: The best way to characterize it is—who knows? Because at this point, Emmanuel Macron has been elected President in an Obama-type campaign, with algorithms checking every opinion, and what the more insightful people are saying here is that on one side you have Marine Le Pen, an old-fashioned populist, and on the other you have the e-populism of Emmanuel Macron. Macron's campaign played on bottom-up emotions—but in fact, he was promoted since April of last year, with the results that we know. It's like a self-fulfilling prophecy. Who was covered on the covers and pages of the magazines, television, everywhere? Macron and Marine Le Pen. What was planned, finally happened.

So, Macron is now in power. As you know, I am relatively knowledgeable of what he is. He is a banker, and at the same time a pianist; he's also a civil servant. But, the best way to characterize Macron, is to say that he played on everything the international banking system could do to help him. He received the support of Obama, before the election, which is absolutely incredible; it's an interference in the national affairs of France. After the election Obama sent him a video supporting him. [German Finance Minister] Schäuble supported him too.

Solidarité et Progrès

Jacques Cheminade

Macron is somebody who is very nice, very sympathetic with everybody. Everybody, after leaving a meeting with him, thinks he agreed with them on everything. But in fact, he is like a sponge—he absorbs things. Better than that, the best way to characterize the situation is to say that he's a chameleon, which adapts to the universe where he evolves. He picks up the color of the universe wherever he evolves.

I say all that before discussing the Belt and Road Forum with you, because Macron sent Raffarin there. So that may be a good sign, because Raffarin is a former Prime Minister, and in France, he's the official who knows China the best. He has a very good insight into Chinese affairs, he's traveled there many times, and he knows all the Chinese leaders. So in that sense, Macron is going along with the tide.

Also, he appointed Philippe Etienne as his personal diplomatic counselor. He was the ambassador in Berlin before this appointment, and had earlier been deployed at Eastern European and Moscow embassies. He has also been chief of cabinet of right-wing and left-wing governments. So he's a professional.

He was appointed instead of the person who was expected by some, the former French ambassador in Washington, Gérard Arau, who is an arch neocon. So the neocon was not appointed, and the man who was appointed is a professional in diplomatic affairs. Those are two noteworthy things.

Now, the Prime Minister was just appointed, and it's Edouard Philippe. He is the right-hand man of Alain Juppé and formerly closest collaborator of Jacques Chirac at the right-wing party, the UMP.

Emmanuel Macron
@EmmanuelMacron

Macron describes himself as being neither right nor left, as being right *and* left at the same time, because the interests of France are above all that. So, who can predict what the policy will be? If he goes in the direction of Obama, the bankers, Schäuble, and company, it would be a real disaster. But, because he's a chameleon, if there are stronger forces putting pressure on him, he may go to a different direction. But he will not inspire anything; he's a man that goes with the tide.

So, in terms of the Belt and Road, let's see what happens. If the pressure is big enough on the French government and on France, he will not necessarily oppose it. He will not promote it, or play the cards that France should play, but he won't oppose it.

EIR: What are the implications of the fact that he doesn't really have a political party? That he's his own party, in effect?

Who is President Macron?

Cheminade: Well, you have to understand that although he's been elected with more than 65% of the vote, the voters did not vote positively for him, but because they rejected the other candidates, in particular Marine Le Pen. And now, 61% of the French voters expect that he won't have a majority in Par-

Marine Le Pen
CC/Remi Noyon

liament, and that he will have to make a compromise with the moderate right wing. It seems very likely so, because he appointed Edouard Philippe, who was a former collaborator of Juppé. You have to understand also that Juppé was connected with [former French Prime Minister Michel] Rocard in the past. They wrote a book together. So this is the Rocard side of Macron.

Macron is very aware of the crisis of the financial system; he's probably one of the French politicians who is the most aware of it. But at the same time, for his career, he decided to play the games of the banks—that was the implication of our discussions. He said, if you don't play the games of the banks you can't succeed.

So, now that he has succeeded, I don't know what he will do.

He's very clever, you see. Like a very clever young boy—he has some insight into some things. He should not be overestimated, of course, but he should not be underestimated either.

I didn't not vote for him. I put in a blank vote, which is neither for one nor the other. The debate between Marine Le Pen and him was a real embarrassment for France. It was a really low-level debate, where she was like a—how would you say this, like an ogress? Like a woman who eats babies. She thought that she could eat Macron, and Macron was like a cold fish that she could not swallow.

So he appeared as moderate, and competent, and so forth, and he won the debate. Even in the right wing of France, people are furious against Marine Le Pen, who lost the debate because she attacked him in an extremely brutal and impotent way. Even her father says Marine Le Pen behaved like a badly educated person.

Politics is volatile, people are walking on their heads, and what will come, who knows? If

Macron follows the policy that he has defined, his rate of approval could drop to 20% by the beginning of November. But who knows? Maybe he will try another policy. Nobody knows what he will do.

That he appointed Raffarin was a surprise. In my communiqué after the second round of the election, I stated that he should give two signals on international policy: First he should go to Beijing. He did not go, because the Belt and Road Forum was the same day as his inauguration. But he sent Raffarin, who is not somebody from his party, not somebody that he knows. But he's the best French politician in terms of his insight into China. And then, at the same time, in the diplomatic game of musical chairs, he appointed somebody who is a professional. So who knows what he has in mind?

His mind is—it's as though he knows the weakness of France, and he wants to create a situation where he can dump the parties; it's a kind of Berlusconi situation, dumping the right wing and the left, as he succeeded in doing. But making the system survive by dumping the parties.

I don't know if it's comprehensible from an American standpoint, because in France, there is no spoils system. In France, you have to go along with your administration. So he's an administration guy at the same time that he's a banker. So you have these two types of identities in the same person.

EIR: One thing I heard from you recently, concerns the great number of individual communications, messages, that you got from Frenchmen during the course of your campaign, and probably since—that indicated a lot. Could you say something about that?

Cheminade: It's funny, because the journalists did not attack me in the way they had done in the past. There were only two very hostile articles, one in *Le Parisien*, naming Lyn [Lyndon LaRouche] and attacking Lyn. Even one of the journalists in a very popular show presented an image of Lyn from a relatively positive standpoint, saying, "this is LaRouche. He said that you are connected to the inside of the country, and you are not connected to the Parisian elites. Do you think LaRouche was right to say that? And what do you think about who should rule France?"

Hundreds of Messages

So we got a very, very poor vote in total. Sixty-five thousand votes was less than in 1995 or 2012. But at the

Xinhua/Lyu Xun

Jean-Pierre Raffarin, President Macron's special envoy to the Belt and Road Forum for International Cooperation, delivering his speech in Beijing on May 14, 2017.

same time, we got these hundreds and hundreds of messages supporting us, saying "your campaign is the best. What you say about culture was excellent," and so on. It's a kind of strange situation, where we're reaching a lot of people.

Now, I will go on a tour of France, a tour of the whole country, to respond to invitations of people who wrote to me. These are theater directors, hospital directors, groups of teachers, groups of youth, even young journalism-school students—three schools of journalism reacted very positively to what we are saying. And what they told me in private was, "we picked up this journalism profession, because we believed in truth. And then we saw, through your campaign, that truth is not respected, so that's why we are interested in you."

We have a lot of that. It's wonderful. At the same time, the official TV channels, except one or two—it's very funny—want to interview me again especially on the water issue—the water needed for Africa and the third world to stop the drought. This involves Alain Gachet—I don't know if you followed it—he is the engineer and entrepreneur who came to our Berlin Schiller Institute conference, and has developed the competence to locate from space the rock formations that can carry water, and then find the aquifers nearby. When I mentioned that, the reporter asked me, "But why is this not done?" and I said, "because people don't care about those that are dying in such countries." So he said, "you should come back on another program after the election."

So there is this type of interest, which is unprecedented. I don't know why—it's difficult to say why. The fact that I had met Macron before, even if I opposed him, impresses people. If you are part of what is on stage, the French are impressed. So it was different from the other times [Jacques' two previous Presidential candidacies in 1995 and 2012]—they were sort of respectful.

The way they tried to eliminate me was to say, "you use very strong words, to say that France is occupied by financial forces. You are comparing that to the Nazi occupation—these are strong words. But you are clever, you are funny, you are a very good person to meet—but, but, obviously, you can't be at the head of a state, or you can't be a politician, because you lack the proper understanding of things!" What they mean in reality is that I lack the corruption to succeed. This what some officials told me. [laughter]

Now, after the elections, it's a funny situation—64,000 people voted for me. So in a discussion with a journalist, who is launching a blog in Paris and who voted for me, I told her that half of them probably are interesting for us and represent the future. She said, "No, no, no! Not half, all of them! Because to vote for you, requires someone really connected to ideas and to the future, and all these people are interesting." And then she added, "But a few million others who did not vote for you" are very interested by what you have to say. We got a lot of messages from people, all of a sudden—that's something you would like because it's very, in a sense, very American, in the way you would think about it.

I met a man coming back from Germany in a place in central France. He looked at me, and said, "but, but, but—y-you're Jacques Cheminade!" I said, "yes." He said, it was like a revelation for him. He had seen me on the screen, and then it was a reality. So, the journalists had tried so hard to make people think it was not a reality, that when they see the reality, it is as though it came out of nowhere! Or like a ghost appearing to him.

Then this person spent at least ten or fifteen minutes talking to me. When I had to leave, he wanted to keep

Solidarité et Progrès

Jacques Cheminade campaigning in Toulouse, France on April 14, 2017.

talking to me about economic issues. "I don't understand anything on economics," he said; "can you explain? You started to do so, but that was not enough, I want to know more. I am a truck driver, and the people from Bulgaria and Romania are ruining my job, but I discuss with them, and they are treated like beasts. I have compassion for them—I don't share what Marine Le Pen says, but at the same time, these foreigners are taking away our jobs. Can you explain to me what's happening?"

So we have a lot of that. Also people are very attracted by what I say on culture. They say, "you have a sense of what culture is," to work for the future, and space, the development of Africa, and transforming the oceans into areas for human development, and not polluting the oceans. That's very good, now we understand how you define it.

So for many of these people, I'm a visionary, but a visionary is not intended to be the head of a state. I hope you understand what I mean.

De Gaulle and Today

EIR: Not yet, but soon. I mean, it may be immodest to raise, but you deliberately recreated the image of de Gaulle when he was addressing the French from London, by saying France is under financial occupation, When he said, "France has lost a battle, France has not lost the war." And to me, you inspired the organic leaders of France who have ...

Cheminade: Yes, but you have to be cautious with this de Gaulle image. Because the French are very bad about taking responsibility and acting like de Gaulle, but they are very good at speaking about de Gaulle. All the candidates said, "I admire de Gaulle." In his inauguration speech, Macron said that de Gaulle had saved

France, and that he would follow what de Gaulle said. He praised de Gaulle, then Pompidou, Mitterrand, Chirac, Sarkozy, and Hollande. [All the Presidents of France in succession.] So you have this confusion about the past.

I have to say, my de Gaulle is the de Gaulle that left on June 1940 for England because he could not stand a locked-in situation. And what the press did in this election—they tried to put in the minds of the people, the idea that the situation was locked in with the Presidential candidates Marine Le Pen and Macron. And so they destroyed François Fillon, for example. Fillon is a Thatcherite, so we cannot cry on his political grave, but at the same time, he was for the rapprochement with Russia. He is a Thatcherite in domestic policies, but he knows Putin very well, and he was close to Putin. So he had to be thrown off the stage.

At the same time, look at Xi Jinping, who was the first to call Macron. The Chinese are very interested in France. I think they understand the situation in France better than the Russians do. So the Russians interviewed me three or four times. They were always interviewing me to explain to them why I was against Marine Le Pen. And I said, "Look, not only is she incompetent, but—she may not be xenophobic herself, but she plays the xenophobia card, and it's very dangerous, because it pits the French Muslims against the other Frenchmen, and this could create a disaster not only in France, but throughout Europe."

So the Russians want explanations, and at this point, I was astonished: I was interviewed in French, in English, and in Spanish! Three languages. [laughter]

EIR: About what happened in the election and what is the situation now, right? That's basically what they wanted to know?

Cheminade: Well, they are Russians, so they understand that they have to work with Macron. They may not like him, but they will try to see what comes out of him. The Chinese, through this Raffarin invitation, are taking the temperature. Everybody is taking the temperature. The problem is, Macron at this point, still has no temperature, so there is nothing to be taken.

He's very cautious also—you have to understand the person. He's extremely cautious. He would compare himself in private to Kennedy. Not to Obama, to Kennedy.

EIR: Oh, really?

Cheminade: Of course. He's a narcissist, so he thinks he did it by himself, that people helped him—okay, they helped him; he's a pragmatist, he's practical, and he got advantages from them. But, he believes that he himself did it. By himself. He's this type of person. So that's the situation today.

And France is losing its industry. It is losing the level of public education, all the things that were part of the "French exception," which was the public health system, public education, and also more or less directed development—all of these are evaporating. For example, today there are at least two or three Frances: There's the France of the metropolis, of the big cities; then the France of the rural world; and then the in-between. And people work—it's like in Los Angeles, if you made a comparison to the United States—Paris is full of money and people who work in Paris cannot pay for a house around Paris. So sometimes they're 150 km, or maybe even 200 km [95 or 125 miles] from Paris, and they travel four or five hours a day to get to work.

So given that situation, most of these people who are enraged, would vote for Le Pen. And the Le Pen party is also divided. There is a Le Pen party in the North, which is pro-working class, strongly social, and even supports the public sector and so on; and the Le Pen party in the South, which is much more xenophobic and liberal. You have a fight between the two, and Marion Maréchal-Le Pen, who is Marine Le Pen's niece, and represented this wing in the South—she decided to opt out of politics! Everybody thinks she got out because she wants to come back. She wants to rally all the right-wing formations, while Marine Le Pen wanted to make it by herself.

So there are big fights in all parties; the Socialist Party is exploding, the Front National has an internal war, the right-wing is exploding; everything is disarticulating in this period of crisis, and Macron appears as a reference, where all the rest are exploding in all directions.

But he can appear as a reference as long as he's not in power. As soon as he's in power, the reference would tend to evaporate!

Why People Are Coming to Us

EIR: Yes. It seems the more important role for *you*, than as—

Cheminade: Yes, right. We have to make it in the interior of the country, where there are the best reactions. What's also interesting is the reactions of the second or third generation of people who came to

France, people mainly from Africa, but not only, who said, "you understand the world, the others don't." I was very struck by something that was said in the discussion inside our movement: there are not only the common objectives of humanity, but the common emotions of humanity. So a lot of people coming to us, come on the basis of an emotion connected to the destiny of the Universe. That's what they have in mind. And they say that the others have only concerns for the destiny of their immediate belongings.

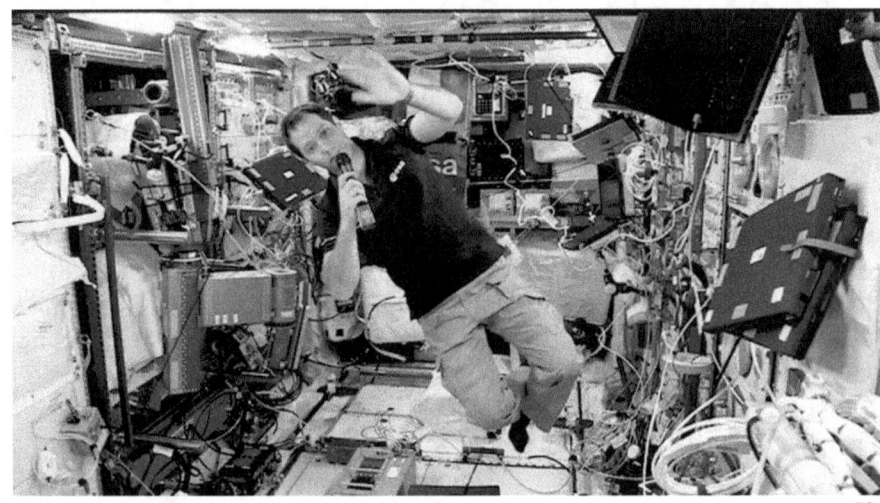
ESA
Thomas Pesquet talks to the European press from space.

For example, we had a very interesting case, dramatic, but very interesting: He's a friend of ours who leads a chorus in eastern France. His best friend is a young entrepreneur working with him in the chorus, as a cultural effort that they are organizing together. His friend was supposed to vote for me. But coming back from the polls, he told him—"I am ashamed; I am ashamed, and I feel so bad." His friend asked, "Why?" He said, "I went to the polls with two ballots, one for Cheminade and the other for Macron. And finally, I voted for Macron, because Macron represented stability for me over the next five years. Where Cheminade represents the future. But I want my firm to succeed, so I finally voted for Macron instead of Cheminade, and I am so ashamed."

EIR: Right! That's incredible! That's wonderful.

Cheminade: The other thing I want to stress is that people did not vote for foreign policy issues. They were not part of the campaign—which is a scandal, because a French President first has to deal with that. They recognized that we were stressing these issues—the New Silk Road, relations with Russia, and the world role that France would play because France is a permanent member of the UN Security Council.

So this was not considered in the vote. But now, it is being considered! Which means that people feel more free now, after the vote, than before the vote, to be interested in what really matters.

EIR: Can you say something about your campaign on the issues of space exploration, space travel.

Cheminade: Oh, well, I'm known—people that want to slander me, say "the lunar candidacy."

EIR: Yeah, "he wants to go to Mars," I know.

Cheminade: "To conquer space." So I said, listen, it's not to conquer space, it's to explore it, because if human beings don't explore, they are imbeciles. And I also said that the French astronaut who is on the International Space Station (ISS), Thomas Pesquet, is studying how to better struggle against nosocomial diseases in hospitals, and about echography at a distance. So, he's not going into space for tourism; he's going into space to organize things which are useful on the Earth, to see how it works there, so that mankind then will be able to advance beyond the present into the future. Because it exists, it's very useful for everybody to know what it is, as a human being: Destiny is that, to explore space.

So it's very funny because a friend of ours, Jean-Pierre Luminet who is one of the best known experts in space, published the French translation of Edgar Allan Poe's *Eureka* as a single book with his own introduction. He called the book, *Eureka: The Universe According to Edgar Poe.* I've read it, and his attacks against Bacon and Aristotle are violent, and at the same time he praises, as you know, Kepler as the only one having a consistent conception, starting from the unity of the Universe and not from fractions of the Universe. So it's very funny for the French to have that in front of their noses, because it's against the British ideology. And the effects of the British occupation of France may not be to be pro-British, but to be against anything that appears to be challenging the rules of the game.

EIR: Right! That's interesting. And there's a world

revival right now. I'm getting emails about that piece of Edgar Allan Poe's, *Eureka*. It's circulating, and maybe in part because of your campaign. They're discussing it just as you described, all over the world right now, maybe among other things because of your campaign.

People Know Helga Zepp-LaRouche

Cheminade: Well, people know in France that Helga [Zepp-La-Rouche] was the author or the inspirer of the New Silk Road. These people know that, at this point. They know it because we had the Schiller conference here two years ago in Paris. So, it's known, but it is not said, and what you have to understand is that it's known, but by what, 10, 15% of the population. At least 50% don't even know my name. Because they're not interested in politics. Part of the population, like in the United States, or even probably worse, is out of politics. As soon as they hear the word "politics" on television, they turn the sound down. So they don't know me.

And as you know very well, a lot of people talk to me in the street. When I go there, they say, "what you did was good, wonderful." I ask, "did you vote for me?" "No, this time, no, but next time." [laughter] I am known: At least our ideas are known for what they are. The slander that this space guy is crazy— working with little green men, and so on—absolutely evaporated.

And also the attacks against Lyn, except in two cases. Because we published a lot on our website, on our understanding, and an account of my meetings with Lyn and what it meant. So, these days, they don't dare to attack. What they are saying now, is that I don't exist. The Anglo-American press, or the British press, pretend I don't exist. In the big debate, for example of the eleven candidates [on April 4], they said that I was "out of it," against several hundred messages saying "you did the right thing, you attacked who needed to be attacked, it was good."

So what they set up in this presidential debate, was a candidate called "Philippe Poutou"—I don't know if you have heard of him, probably not. He's a Trotskyist, and he attacked Marine Le Pen and Fillon saying, "you

Solidarité et Progrès

Presidential Candidate Jacques Cheminade, in a webcast campaign meeting on April 18, 2017.

avoided a summons from the judges, but I myself, a poor worker, if the judges call me I have to go, or go to jail," blah, blah, blah. Later he was promoted by *Le Monde* as the one who won the debate, and he was also promoted by the *New York Times*, which was funny. And this guy was set up to attack Fillon and Marine Le Pen, and therefore to promote Macron.

So it's a fake democracy. It's not only a democracy without a Republic, but it's a fake democracy. A simulacrum of democracy.

But at the same time, there are a lot of people—I was in Nancy for example, with a few people, and there was even a priest among them. It's a Christian milieu, and they all said, "you changed our lives, because we have taken distance from these things—before, we had no understanding about the world." So you have a lot of that, coming from very little, very small groups, and also at the same time, these two, three, four or five million people—who knows?—who are interested in what we are saying.

EIR: Thank you so much. That's wonderful.

Cheminade: It is, but it's not enough. Because the challenge is ahead of us, and the work starts now. And some people are discouraged at the fact that we received so few votes. They say, we worked for a year and a half—and we have so little votes. But now it's being overcome, and we are removing ahead with unprecedented potential.

EIR: Thank you so much.

MAN'S TRUE INTENTION!

How the Future Builds Its Past

by Lyndon H. LaRouche, Jr.

August 4, 2013 occurred in the week when the British Empire's J.P. Morgan virtually declared war against what was then formally identified as the firm's choice of mortal foe: **which was us**. *Our quarrel on that account, is not among a collection of some more or less numerous individuals, or even some particular nation; it is now our battle to save civilization from the most evil agency in the world today: the actions of the imperial forces of the Anglo-Dutch world-empire and its effects on the future. The issue is still a world empire under the reign of Britain's malicious Elizabeth II who is the actually avowed principal enemy-in-fact of our own U.S. republic.*

In this conflict, the principle of this present defense of our republic, must be traced properly in recent world history: as traced now from the leadership which had been associated with the Great Golden Renaissance's Nicholas of Cusa, and, also, later, Cusa's follower, Johannes Kepler in the matter of the deeply rooted principles of physical science. Cusa and Kepler still represent the same principles of physical science which the great dramatist William Shakespeare demonstrated in the particular case of the "Chorus" introduced in Shakespeare's **King Henry V**: *the same common heritage of the greatest Classical dramas and Classical composers of music, poetry, and of what should also be known as physical science. Let your future create your past!*

Commonwealth Heads of Government

The malicious Empress Elizabeth, "the actually avowed principal enemy-in-fact of our own U.S. republic," shown here presiding over her Empire, at the November 2009 Commonwealth Heads of Government meeting in Trinidad and Tobago.

Foreword
These Higher Principles

The search for any actually truthful insight into the matters to which I have just pointed immediately above, must overcome those systemic difficulties which tend to block the pathway to rediscovery of the actual meaning of truth for what is presently identified as "physical science," as that science was properly understood by such exceptional minds as those of Nicholas of Cusa and Johannes Kepler, and, perhaps, much earlier, the water of Heraclitus' science, too. Unfortunately, present academic and contingent sets of educational practices, have lately tended to discard the high standard for science which had been that such as what Max Planck and Albert Einstein had represented in their time. Whereas, their opponents from the ranks of the late Twentieth and early Twenty-first centuries, have tended toward the brutishly crude, ideological practices, practices which have polluted what had been formerly the honorable, scientific classrooms, now supplanted by the thuggery of Bertrand Russell's legacy.

True scientists, especially great ones, think actually within the setting of the future, rather than the past. Do you?

The opposition to which I have just referred, above, is the effect of the general lack in the ability of most people of the relatively same rank today: their typical inability to summon from among themselves, that crucial knowledge needed to recognize the intrinsic fallacy of present-day, so-called "popular opinion" as such. What I mean by that, is that the error which must be recognized, is to be located in that intrinsic fallacy which a brutish sort of contemporary opinion on the subject of "sense-perception," typifies. *Thus: Among the relatively few best scientific thinkers of modern times, there had been the still very relevant Bernhard Riemann, who, in writing the concluding sentence of his 1854 habilitation dissertation, made a proper distinction in his separating what are meaningfully true universal physical principles, as to be distinguished from what were merely a class of empirical deductions from an assorted collection of mere sense-perceptions as such.*

The origin of the failures in science which confront us here and now, has been more a blinded soul's reliance on the systemic fallacy and trap of merely currently immediate sense-perception, a trap which has been used as a virtually categorical substitute for what is the necessary action of real science. That often remains a distraction, which, in this way, has tended to make a true insight into actual principles nearly impossible, as by pre-emption, and, to turn what should have been heroes, into opportunists, by intention.

The choice between folly and victory, is, thus, to be secured by the separation of true physical principles from what were merely the constructs of credulous, gambling fools. True principles, like those of Riemann, have been typified with a nice elegance in the discoveries of principles such as those made by such as Max Planck and Albert Einstein. Competent science, and true victory, alike, are to be found only "outside" any merely mathematical deductions—in these awful days, *science today exists only in the making of the future.*

Only fools gamble, as Alexander Hamilton could have told you, had he still lived.

The Problem with Mere Mathematics

The effort to delimit notions of principles to merely methods of mathematical concoctions, tends toward producing a deadly exclusion of any true notion of an actually universal physical principle; it is, in fact, a virtual practice of the veritable witch-doctors and gamblers gathered on Wall Street's **Boardwalk**.

When today's practice of what is named science recognizes the inherent fallacy of what passes for the blind worship of a "conventional mathematics," better identified as "gambling" in empty air; today's calamitous trends in a popular science, and "business," too, must re-discover the human mind from an earlier century of such senior figures from the 1890s as Planck and Einstein: to learn from them, what are, still, really, the necessary foundations of a true physical science. By a true physical science, I mean a science which lives in the actual future, and, therefore, one created by persons whose minds, also, already live in their actual future.

The downward-going, devil's difference made from the likes of Bertrand Russell, to which I had just referred immediately above, was already prominently reigning in the then prevalent trends of the 1920s, then in a time when I had been born, and, then, still beyond. The difference in what passes, unfortunately, for a true standard of science, has come to be typified by the ration of those then-currently prominent physicists and chemists, such as those of the life-time of a President Franklin Roosevelt, *who would defend* our *republic* against the typically, utterly fraudulent, implicitly "green," British hoax-craft of the likes of such as the dupes who followed the image of the silly Isaac Newton.

Success in Forecasting

Take an example of this issue of distinctions: take, for example, the common folly of attempts to define *an a-priori distinction of "life" from "non-life," by using those terms of merely mathematical arguments which have been often mistaken for "truth" by the overly zealous.* Or, for example: consider the savagely destructive delusion which is produced by the pretext of treating the subject of an actual matter of a physically efficient principle in forecasting, by a resorting to mathematical deductions derived from a merely presumed human knowledge of principles measured in past purely mathematical clock-times. *The ability to adduce a truly universal physical principle, must be prescribed, instead, as requiring the developed ability to present a current forecast of **what must be also a quality of that true foresight which goes intrinsically into a true sense of an actual future which actually exists only beyond the alleged "powers" of mere sense-perception, but, which, rather, exists only within the actual process of generating a future!***

EIRNS/Stuart Lewis

Successful cases of forecasting "have occured in their most familiar form of expression as 'presciences': they occur, in my experience, as like an effect of 'tuning-in on' a fortuitous stepping into a what may have seemed to have been a sensation from a broadcast 'heard as streaming from my head into the future.'" Here, LaRouche presents his famous "Triple Curve" function, January 1998.

For example: in relatively customary cases, there is a very limited ability to forecast an actual change in principle of action, insofar as my own experiences with frequently successful forecasting experiences, have often successfully demonstrated. "Experiencing an unexpected development," which had occurred in the course of forecasting a development of that type, occurs among some persons, **but never actually occurs "as if deductively."**

My experience with the most frequent instances of successful cases of forecasting the future, including my own future, have happened to have been chiefly in the relative domain of economy. Those successful cases have occurred in their most familiar form of expression as "presciences": they occur, in my experience, as like an effect of "tuning-in on" a fortuitous stepping into what may have seemed to have been a sensation from a broadcast "heard as streaming from my head into the future." The experience "appears" in the guise of "an ebb and flow in a heightened effect of a generally maturing awareness" of the future.

The proper function of the human mind, is to create a fresh new existence which dwells within the actualized future.

However, there is never anything "magical" in such experiences of forecasting; it occurs "as an actual foreseeing of" an experience of an approaching, oncoming awareness, and can, implicitly, be consciously brought forth by a form of concentration experienced as of an "on-coming" quality, as in the likeness of a sense akin to approaching changes in weather. The cases of both Max Planck and Albert Einstein illustrate the point.

Doubters aside, such forecasts have occurred, as in instances of my own experience, and really do occur, as according to my personal experience, in the degree that they are to be experienced, when considered retrospectively, as validatable experiences *which had actually been occurring before the sensed fact*. I have experienced a relatively few, but nonetheless notable such instances of a quality of remarkable experiences which qualify as having been compelling certainties. I mean certainties which fit the image of the "certainties" of an actual forecast which has more or less global importance, as that aroused in shaping a turnabout in the course of human experience on a broad scale. It merely occurs to be the case that most of my such experiences of importance, do fit within the category of crucially important economic effects on a scale of national or even greater importance. It can be observed with little difficulty, that I now do that much of the time, that done simply as needed "in the course of business."

What this variety of my own now long-standing experience shows, principally, is that the conventional outlook of people engaged with certifiably important implications in practice, is such, that the cultural characteristics of most among even exceptionally influential persons and circles, however relatively credible otherwise, often fall far short of such a customary experience among even what are usually considered exceptionally able social strata. *They should have been made capable of foreseeing*, as I have observed this frequently in my own work; but, instead, most among them had failed to exercise that capability, even on fairly impor-

While even the most influential people fail when it comes to forecasting, "MacArthur's decision at Inchon demonstrates the case of the truly leading type of creative personalty (it was Harry S Truman who had things bass-ackwards)."

tant occasions, even crucial ones, as General Douglas MacArthur's decision at Inchon demonstrates the case of the truly leading type of creative personalty (it was Harry S Truman who had things bass-ackwards). The state of corruption of what had been competently trained scientists, has often not been the outcome of failed attention to a competent science; it is folly which seeks silly solace in some set of popular opinions.

The "lesson to have been learned," should now be made necessarily clear, as follows:

I
Sense Perception: the Hoax

Most among the common frauds presented in the mere name of science, as conventionally typified by the cases of Euclid and Aristotle, are rooted in the *a-priori* expressions (e.g., "past," "post hoc") of what is an actually extremely dubious, and wholly fictitious, mere presumption of the arbitrary form of existence of such a geometry *per se*. A related sort of hoax is foisted, similarly, respecting the origins of the notion of life; that same hoax, is also foisted, a-priori, on both the existence

of life itself, and also the principle of the human mind.

From those persons listed as bringing home wretched mere presumptions, the hoaxsters responsible for the elements of that strange listing, have fashioned the sheer hoax against the very existence of that unique specificity of the human mind which is lacking in all other known living species. That is to emphasize the crucial feature of human existence, in contrast to all known types of other living species, which shows the unique process of increasing the energy-flux density of the human species, as that increase is expressed through man's simple use of fire and beyond, toward the higher levels of nuclear fission, thermonuclear fusion, then matter-antimatter, and, then, beyond that.

The problematic issue amid all this, is the inherent failings which must be attributed to human psychological dependency upon the habit of "mere sense-perception."

There is nothing "inherently wrong" in the use of sense-perception itself. The problem lies with what is merely that. The problematic feature is located efficiently in the limits which reliance upon a merely bare sense-perception imposes, intrinsically. That is not "a fault" of sense-perception, excepting in respect to the limitations which mankind incurs in relying on such a medium as a virtually self-evident basis for the practice of human knowledge. Man often makes himself a fool, but only if he treats the medium of sense-perception as it were an outer limit of the natural talent for scientific knowledge.

There is much more to this matter, as shall now follow.

The higher authority is located, most typically, in the media of truly "Classical artistic" practice. William Shakespeare's creation of his character "Chorus," in **King Henry V**, is among the many repeatable instances of what are rightly distinguished as those media which typify the human mind's power to rise above the impoverished media of sense-perception in the latter's biological-functional expressions. Classical musical composition and its appropriate expressions, only typifies the human mind's super-imposition over the mere level of biology in the domain, in which life supersedes, by the margin of a virtual universe, the mean limitations of mere chemistry.[1]

Or, to restate the point in a somewhat more refined expression, "life" is the superior medium which has transcended mere chemistry; the notion of life, as dis-

---

1. Compare my "Nicholas of Cusa, Kepler & Shakespeare," June 10, 2013, in EIR, June 21, 2013, or LaRouchePAC.

tinct from mere chemistry, and as the superiority of human life to merely animal life: all such as those bespeak those relevant domains to which I am turning your attention here. Cardinal Nicholas of Cusa's **De Docta Ignorantia** reaches that level of a distinctive specific intention respecting the highest reach of human intention this far.

Those points of distinction are the prerequisites for the human species' capability of actually reaching from beyond Earth as such, into the necessity of man's intellectual entry into domains beyond the modest limits of the merely biological chemistry of life in general on Earth. With that action, mankind reaches, even efficiently, from beyond the fools' domain of what were merely sense-perception. It is, notably, the superior domain of the human mind which, alone, renders mankind something above "mere Earthlings," if we are willing to try, and, then, succeed.

With those words now spoken, I will have sought to turn your attention to places beyond the neighboring planets and, sooner or later, stars. Now, having said so much this far, follow me in what now follows as man among the stars: as I once wrote in a poem titled "*My Lyre*," about sixty years ago: *". . . bending stars like reeds."*

What Is Wrong with 'Sense Perception'

In consistency with what I have outlined as some crucial considerations in my argument this far, the serious qualities of thinking of the human being are located in what had not been actually experienced this far. It is, therefore, necessary to pre-think what one is about to experience, that as what one is about to think. My observations on my experience with public school-room classes and kindred circumstances, had led me, not uncommonly, to be aware of an un-trustworthy characteristic of the school room. The result was often my stubborn resistance to what I recognized as an attempt to force my attention to be focused on arguments which I considered what we today would identify as "spin." My defense-tactic in cases where a kind of instinctive rejection of apparent "manipulation"

The hoax of sense perception: "Most among the common frauds presented in the mere name of science" are typified by the cases of Euclid and Aristotle. . . ." Euclid (left), and Aristotle, as portrayed by Raphael in the "School of Athens" (1509).

was in progress, as during my early adult manhood, had drawn me to think in "Classical poetic" or like veins, as a means of defense against the unwanted intrusions emanating from the classroom and its like.

The result of that is reflected, typically, in my "Nicholas of Cusa, Kepler & Shakespeare."[2] The Classical mode in drama, Classical music, and poetry, was the source of the influence and bulwark of my intellectual defense against unwanted categories of intrusions. This included prominently, my disgust with the efforts to gain my submission to the hoaxes of Euclid and Aristotle. Fortunately, my fascination with the constructions in progress at the Charlestown Navy Yard (in a suburb of Boston at the verge of my adolescence), armed me against Euclid's hoax. The Classical modalities prevailed upon me on most accounts then; this was a part of a crucial point in the entire sweep of my life from the time of early grades in a local grammar school, onwards. The fact is, that that experience and my commitment to it, "saved my mind." This prevailed in all categories of the educational and closely related considerations. I look back to that experience as having been the "defense of my mind" against the standard curricula. It is not what you appear to think, but the way in which you think it, which is ultimately decisive in crafting what you become. "Practical" is for me, a called alert to do battle. Classmates who did not resist

_____
2. Ibid.

as I would do on account of the Classical principle, left me with the feeling that I was being betrayed by my friends, or, perhaps an experience of going into a better profession. Hence, my periods of devotion to the wonderful consolations provided by Classical artistic compositions generally. There was, and is, a very clear distinction in what some would term "styles," in all that.

When you might have taken to heart what I have just written this far, you have fair access to an outlook on my practices and their underlying motivations. Among all features of that world-outlook which I have just referenced on my own account, the Classical repertoire of categories, including that of Nicholas of Cusa, Johannes Kepler, Classical poetry, Classical drama, and Classical music, exemplify who and what I am in that to which I am the most devoted, including the love for the very idea of what mankind should be able of becoming.

However, the heart of it all is my devotion to participation in the future: what mankind should be capable of becoming. Now it is time to become very serious.

II
Walking Inside the Future

Insofar as we know presently, the human species is the only form of life which has the capability of foreknowledge of future events and related developments. A very much smaller fraction of that total human population has shown active insight into the implications of that fact. Nonetheless, despite the latter fact of the present situation, the fact that some living human persons manifest such a capability with significant facility, is sufficient to define that capability as being a universal principle of our said species.

The crucial distinction of those actively prescient of their own such capability, is that they have some significant degree of actual knowledge of the practical implications of the special intellectual capabilities involved. Hence, I identify such persons as "Walking Inside The Future."

That much now said here, the crucially significant characteristic of witting participants in such knowledge, is that they are enabled to exhibit a conscious awareness of the "special characteristics" of the experiencing of conscious apprehension of the distinctive features of the experiencing of that process, as

distinct from merely ordinary recollections of past experiences. The unwitting person, may stand outside the door, but does not knock to enter; the witting person knocks, at the least, and may actually open the door.

Those admittedly rare such forecasters, tend to shift emphasis from treating foreknowledge as a shadow cast, to active interrelations with the creative process as an active faculty accompanying what might be considered as recent experience. This does not occur as in the sense of a delivered message, but as a process of experiencing something "which is running as if 'just ahead of,'" the actually experienced developments in progress. I am personally familiar with the latter quality of experiences with human foresight.

Hence: "Walking inside the moving future."

The relatively greatest of known "fore-seers" insofar as I have been made aware of such a trait, will tend to see a discovery of principle, not as a past event, but as an ongoing one moving just ahead of the process. I trace such developments in terms of on-going processes of discovery. Notably, all of my significant economic and related forecasts, overlap the processes of experience and of prescience.

III
On Background

It should be known among the literate generally, that one's sense of personal identity is shaped, to a more or less greater degree by the changes in the sense of the significance of the person's notion associated with the quality of the role, and associated sense of responsibility, into which they are being, and have been drawn into playing in life over time. In my own case, this had been the strongly-sensed applicable factor in the shaping of my world-outlook into the period of World War II, and some years beyond. It was also what had prompted me to compose some poetry, because such poetry proffered the experiencing of the relevant prototype of creativity. My being drawn into a role in management consulting experiences, later, had set off my accelerating role as an executive in the profession, and into what became my leading role as what has been demonstrated as my ability to have been a leading expert, in the matter of economic forecasting.

Consequently, therefore, to restate appropriately what I had just stated in the foregoing paragraph, the

Ford Motor Co.

LaRouche's forecast of the crash of the "great U.S. auto industry of the 1950s," was the first in a series of comparable forecasts which he has supplied over the decades since, up until the present time. Shown: A Ford assembly line, 1957, Lorain, Ohio.

beginning of "an awareness of myself" as emerging in the role as being in a leading position as a forecaster, emerged from my career in management consulting. The notable event, on this account, was my precise forecast to occur during that time, for an outbreak within the range of a few days of variability for the crash of the "great U.S. auto industry of the 1950s." It was, for me, a crucially unique success as a professional at that time, and, as a matter of the facts of the case, a uniquely successful forecast which I had made in defiance of the failed conclusions supplied by my putative Wall Street-related rivals on that account. It was, otherwise, to be the first of a series of comparable forecasts which I have supplied over the decades later, through to the present time.

Probably, the most notable of such forecasts of mine was my August, 1971 forecast of the great crash of the 1970s, which quickly turned out to have been the greatest post-1929 "crash" in the trans-Atlantic international experience. Today, the world at large, is now being gripped, very soon, by the greatest breakdown-crisis, measured in global effects, in modern world history up to the present date.

However, that does not mean that we are necessarily nearing "the end of the world."[3] My outlook, whether during the late 1970s, or today, was, and remains that of a prospect for bringing civilization out of what has now become this presently monstrous crisis, a crisis which I know could be brought under control, if an appropriate effort were made soon enough, now— while the actual time available is, admittedly, most painfully short.

Consider Some Key Consequences

The immediate danger of "end of the world" options, now, would be that of a general, "globally-extended, imperial warfare," a war which were to be launched at the prompting of the general command under the control of the broad range of the presently existing Anglo-Dutch empire, the empire featuring the current Queen of England, Elizabeth II, or, of her successor. This would be as updated on the present world's calendar, according to a model made in the spirit of the original Roman Empire. That would be the prospective basis for a global thermonuclear-warfare, which is, admittedly, a seriously nearby threat which I concede for this presently immediate time. That Queen has a current, and a practically very loud and persisting commitment to an early reduction of the Earth's human population, to about one billion persons, or much less, instead of what had been earlier, the currently estimated, approximately, seven billions; I am presuming here, that the outcome could be thwarted, as the relevant, U.S. Army General Martin E. Dempsey, so far, has continued to seek to bring that about.

Against that background, the early re-establishment of the original Glass-Steagall Act in the United States at this time, would probably lead to an avoidance of thermonuclear warfare. Otherwise there would be, admit-

---

3. At the present moment, the sudden arrival of the "end of the world" is actually a possibility, but without the real risk of an early, global thermonuclear war, that were not a likely outcome. Very bad things are now possible, but a general thermonuclear bombardment, is something still very much to be prevented, as the U.S.A.'s General Martin Dempsey has rightly emphasized.

tedly, no pre-assured avoidance of a thermonuclear holocaust, or, an actual such holocaust beyond question.

That consideration of the Glass-Steagall restoration thus considered, a prospective renaissance of the U.S. nation and its economy, is a presently feasible outcome. However, otherwise, the incumbency of U.S. Presidents under the 2001-2013 terms, if continued beyond the presently immediate period ahead, is quite probably the determinant of "a human extinction prospect." One might make the point: "The patience of the Creator would be sorely tried."

However, once that much has been said, the actual issue to be considered here, is the question, whether it were likely, or not, that the very early re-installation of the original Glass-Steagall could promptly occur now.

Already, the accelerating trend, since the election of President John F. Kennedy, had been set by the assassination of that President, and, the continuation of that development actually expressed by the assassination of his brother, prospective President Robert Kennedy. Those two murders set on the stage of 1960s U.S. history, remain existent within the deployment of a continuing state of extended warfare spreading throughout the world in one or another expression, an implicitly global spread of global fire through to the present moment as I am writing here and now. It has been a state of threatened warfare since the nuclear warfare threatened by the combinations of such Administrations as those of Britain's Prime Minister Winston Churchill, Bertrand Russell, and the administration of the U.S.A.'s President Harry S Truman; it was a war called off, temporarily, when the British empire discovered that the Soviet Union had a nuclear warfare capability comparable to that of the U.S.A. and the British monarchy; Britain and Bertrand Russell moved on, then, toward thermonuclear warfare. The assassination of U.S. President John F. Kennedy, was promptly used as a pretext for launching a decade of warfare in Indo-China, and then, beyond and beyond, still today. This has now brought us, through the British-Saudi launching of the 9-11 attacks on the United States, to the virtual, present threshold of global thermo-nuclear warfare.

The successful restoration of Glass-Steagall in the U.S.A. now, would signal *an almost-certain-avoidance* of thermo-nuclear warfare. It would also portend the beginning of the launch of an accelerating rate of economic recovery within our United States (in particular).

Fire! The Principle of Progress

Now take under consideration certain broader and deeper considerations, most of which usually pass as either overlooked, mis-conceived, or both.

The exact measure of the continuing existence of the human species, the distinction which distinguishes all mankind from the relatively lower forms of life, has been and remains, most simply defined, the rate of increase of the primary energy-flux density; per capita, and per unit of territory of concentration of human existence of the human species. This also takes under consideration: the rate of that progress so measured.

Among the worst diversions of members of the human population, is the failure to take into effective account, the whole of the process of human existence, a failure demonstrated by concentration on "selected factors," rather than the process as a whole process.

Then comes a more deeply rooted failure in human opinion generally: the "wild-eyed error" of belief, of a popular reliance on sense-perception as such: sense-perception foolishly considered as being a physical principle of measure within the Solar system as such. This should have brought to our intention what should have been the most readily demonstrated, worst systemic fallacy of popular opinion of them all: *the reductionist's human sense-certainty!*

The proper retort against "sense-certainty," is the function of human relationships within the setting of the relevant process of interactions among processes as wholes. That is already "marked-out" for our attentions in the domain of a strictly defined range of *Classical-artistic composition* when considered in terms of processes, as Heraclitus or Plato, Nicholas of Cusa and Johannes Kepler, might have preferred, rather than merely individual parts as treated as the chronic, madly-mathematical reductionist's "merely imaginary infinitesimal" "purely mathematical" grinding of individual species of parts.

The first principle of any competent scientist (in particular), is the reality of human experience! Overlook that, and you are susceptible to believing almost anything that some certain lunatic magician wishes you to believe. The name of the disease I am attacking here, is what is called "reductionism," which is otherwise to be known as the most commonplace expression of what is, unfortunately, the most popular form of systemic human insanity. That is why mathematicians tend to be morally and otherwise insane, as monetarists' thoughts almost always are, or absolutely worse.